Eating Nails for Breakfast

A MEMOIR

Chrissy Liu

For the girls who felt like they were never enough, for the women who still do, and for my daughter, so she never has to.

To my daughter: You are my greatest gift.

"We repeat what we don't repair."

- Christine Langley-Obaugh

Table of Contents

Author's Note

This is a memoir, and memory is subjective. While I have tried to recount events as accurately as possible, others may remember things differently.

To protect privacy, I have changed names and identifying details. In some cases, I have created composite characters or compressed timelines. Conversations have been recreated from memory to capture the essence of what was said, not verbatim transcripts.

The emotional truth of this story is real. The feelings, insights, and journey described are authentically mine.

Prologue: *The Ashes*

I woke up late, 6:30am, fighting off a cold and still a little groggy from the NyQuil. My ringer was off so I didn't hear the alarm or the eight missed calls. One of the calls was from the nursing home, the other seven from my brother. He and I aren't close, so I knew before I even listened to the voicemails.

"Chrissy, this is Nurse Robin from Southpines. I know it's super early, but I wanted to let you know your mom passed away overnight. I'm sorry for your loss but it's a blessing."

It is a blessing. She wasn't wrong.

My mom didn't want a funeral. She hated the idea of people gawking at her dead body in the same funeral home where my dad, her sister, her mom, her dad, and so many more family members were laid out before their funerals. Secretly, I was relieved because a funeral would've meant flying back to Pittsburgh and sitting in a nearly empty funeral home and church. Most of our family was dead, and the few friends my parents had left, she'd alienated in the years since my dad died.

Eight days later her ashes arrived in a USPS priority box from the funeral home in Massachusetts. Human remains tape was wrapped around the box. I was supposed to sign for her ashes, but the postal worker didn't even ring the doorbell, he just dropped it on the porch and left. He probably wanted to avoid what would no doubt be an awkward exchange.

I stood in my husband's office with scissors, hands shaking, cutting through that tape. Inside the box was another box, and inside that was a bag of ashes. My mother had been reduced to something I had to shove into an urn, and it wasn't even something I'd keep in my house. It had to be shipped back to Pittsburgh to be buried alongside my dad.

Irwin sat beside me as I flipped the urn over, opened the seal, and tried to put her ashes in. The bag wouldn't fit. I kept pushing it down, terrified the plastic would rip open and send ashes flying across the room. I could hear Irwin sucking in a breath every time he thought I was stuffing them in too hard. My fear combined with his prompted me to start sobbing.

I was an orphan now.

Both of my parents were gone. I had no one left to call for advice, and I had no one to ask what I was like as a kid when my daughter asks me years from now. There were no grandparents for my daughter.

I finally got the bag in and sealed the urn. For a few moments I just sat there on the floor of Irwin's office, holding a container of my mother's ashes. I waited to feel something bigger, some huge wave of grief, but it didn't come. I mostly felt tired.

Ever since my dad died 12 years prior, my mom had become a shell of her former self. I'd already lost her, and this just made it official. It was just my brother and me, rarely speaking, handling the logistics like a work project.

My mom told me once that if I could count my real friends on one hand in my life, I'd be lucky. I didn't believe her then, or maybe I did and just didn't want to admit it. But it turns out, my mom wasn't very lucky. She died with only one true friend, and in the end, my mom had pushed her away too.

Now, I'm close to 50. My daughter is eight, and I already see so much of me in her. Last week, we took her to celebrate her taekwondo belt test. We were having ice cream to finish off the celebration when a group of girls her age walked in dressed in leotards with bows in their hair, having just finished a dance competition. They were all sitting together, giggling and recounting the morning, and their moms were clustered at another table.

I watched my daughter watching them. She didn't say anything and just kept eating her ice cream. That's what intrigues me, because I can't tell if I'm actually seeing something or if I'm just projecting my own damage onto her.

We are three generations of women who never quite fit in, or maybe it's just me, unable to see anything else. I don't know if I can see her clearly through the lens of my own dysfunction. That's why I'm taking a moment to understand what happened to me, to notice what I continue to carry, so it doesn't get passed down to my daughter. So she'll be protected in ways I wasn't.

I don't want to fuck up my kid any more than I already have. I don't want to repeat the patterns of my parents. But I don't have all the answers, and I'm still figuring it out. And I suspect that may be exactly the point.

Part One:

Learning the Pattern

Chapter 1: *The Tag-Along*

Growing up in the eighties shaped Generation X. We were feral children. We spent most of our childhood outside when we weren't in school, riding bikes around the neighborhood, playing hide and seek, and roaming in loose packs until the streetlights came on.

In the summers, I lived at Woodland Heights, our neighborhood pool, spending long days with a group of girls who were all older than me. We practiced for the swim team, had sleepovers, and laid out slathered in baby oil chasing the perfect tan. When it got too hot, we escaped to the snack bar and charged Bomb Pops and soft pretzels to our parents' tabs.

Some of the older kids called me Chrissy Tornado. I never asked why, but I earned it. I was the youngest and the loudest, the one who cannonballed into the deep end while the older girls were trying to lay out, the one who started water fights nobody asked for. I was always in the mix and always in the way. The girls I spent most of my time with never said anything about my age, but I felt it. I felt the quiet certainty that I didn't quite belong.

For a long time, I told myself the age gap was temporary and that it was something we would all outgrow. But the feeling lingered through the years. I was always half a step behind them, close enough to be included but never fully claimed as part of the core group.

In whoever's house we were in for the sleepover, we ended up in the basement with sleeping bags everywhere. Our nights together involved dark candlelit seances, trying to communicate with anyone from beyond with a Ouija board, and playing light as a feather stiff as a board, where one person lies on the floor while others surround them, repeating the chant as they try to lift the body using just two fingers each. For one sleepover, we decided to step it up and add a lip-syncing contest with costumes and all.

I was nervous because performing wasn't my thing. I didn't mind being loud or wild, but standing up in front of everyone and doing something that was supposed to be cute or sexy felt completely different from starting a water fight. I couldn't for the life of me think of a song to do, and I asked my mom for help. She suggested a Motown song, *My Girl* by the Temptations.

The other girls were doing Bon Jovi, Michael Jackson, or Madonna. I showed up in a long cardigan that hit somewhere around my knees, fully committing to a 1960s aesthetic that no one asked for. I looked like a substitute teacher doing karaoke. The girls cheered me on anyway, which almost made it worse.

There's something particularly humiliating about feeling like you're cheered on out of kindness. I was dying inside. But I finished the song.

Most of the girls at the pool were anywhere from two to six years older than me, but Lauren was different. She was only a few months older, lived a few houses away, and we went to the same school. I'm five years older than my brother, so Lauren became like a sister. Our parents encouraged it, and we were together constantly.

With her, I didn't feel like a tag-along. We were basically the same age and at the same place in life.

Things started to shift in middle school when we both attended a Catholic school in the city. When Lauren and I started there, we were inseparable and quickly absorbed into a group of girls who had all been together since kindergarten. We made friends easily and started spending weekends in the city, moving between each other's houses, hanging out with both seventh and eighth graders, getting to know the guys too. Almost everyone from that school would end up at either the all-boys or all-girls Catholic high school, so it felt like a preview of what was coming. We were all moving in the same direction.

But for the two of us, it was the beginning of something else.

During those years, Lauren and I became especially close with a smaller group of girls. Most weekends were spent all together. Our parents drove us back and forth. We had sleepovers, went to parties, and wasted hours at the mall. We became a tight-knit group, and for the first time, my friendships didn't feel seasonal. They felt like real life, and I actually started to feel like I fit in.

It also didn't take long to see where Lauren landed socially. She was considered one of the prettiest girls in our class, and the guys made that clear. A lot of them had crushes on her, and they always found reasons to talk to her. They paid attention when she walked into a room, and I noticed it because I was standing next to her when it happened.

That's probably when I first realized that I wasn't seen the same way.

I had my first kiss in seventh grade at one of our parties, but the guys were never really interested in me. I was friends with a lot of them. I was athletic and spent recess playing instead of sitting around talking. But those friendships felt like a way to get closer to Lauren, because the guys would ask who she liked or whether she'd be at the weekend party.

Lauren was feminine and soft-spoken, and I wasn't. I came from a loud Italian family where nobody whispered and everybody had an opinion. I had a rougher edge. I argued with the boys, and I once kicked one of them in the balls when he made fun of me. I didn't feel invisible, but I also didn't feel chosen, and each time that feeling stayed a little longer.

The transition to high school was hard for me. Because I'd always been comfortable around guys, being dropped into an all-girls school felt like foreign territory. Even though the all-boys school was across the street and we shared dances, my days were suddenly filled only with girls, and my class in particular was toxic and heavy with cliques. Our middle school group stayed close through freshman year, but as we met more people, that closeness slowly started to loosen.

Toward the end of freshman year, Lauren got a boyfriend. He wasn't someone we'd hung out with before, and along with him came a new group of people. I still went to some parties with her, but that crowd was drinking and I wasn't. It wasn't that I thought I was above it. I just didn't see the appeal, and something about watching everyone get sloppy while I sat there sober made me feel even more like I was on the outside looking in. I started being more selective about where I went and who I was around, partly by choice and partly because I didn't know how to fit in.

By sophomore year, Lauren still had the same boyfriend, and I was being left behind more and more, sometimes by her and sometimes by me. There was one night she went to a party and I stayed home. She called afterward and told me everything, who hooked up with who, who disappeared into bedrooms. Some people were having sex now. I was still occasionally kissing boys, still without a boyfriend, and I was on the outside of whatever was happening. After we hung up, I cried myself to sleep, feeling something I couldn't quite name yet, only that she was already slipping away and I didn't know how to follow.

My athletic build made me stand out in the wrong way. In the eighties and nineties, skinny was beautiful, and I was not skinny. I had thick thighs and a muscular frame from years of sports.

Other girls rolled up their uniform skirts to show more leg, but I didn't.

The bus ride to school was an hour each way, twice a day. It was a small bus, maybe fifteen of us total, with boys from the all-boys school and girls from the all-girls school all thrown together because we lived in the same area.

The girls wore uniforms with plaid skirts, white button-downs, and navy blazers. The boys had their version with khaki slacks, ties, and shirts untucked by the afternoon. The bus was one of the places where we were actually together, and our driver didn't give a shit what we said or did on our rides to and from school.

That afternoon the conversation on the bus was about a few girls in our class who had gotten in trouble for rolling their skirts up. All the girls did it. You'd fold the waistband once or twice before school, hike the hem higher, then let it fall back down before the first bell. It was all about being seen by boys.

Lauren rolled her skirt every day because she had the legs for it. I didn't roll mine. I told myself I didn't care, that I wasn't that kind of girl. But the truth was I was self-conscious.

Damon was sitting across from me, legs stretched out, already performing for whoever was watching. He was the kind of guy who was known for saying whatever came into his head, and you laughed so you didn't become the next target.

He looked at Lauren, then at me, and laughed.

"Please," he said, loud enough for everyone to hear. "No one wants to see your skirt rolled up with that cellulite on your thighs." He smirked. "You look like a cow in that uniform."

My face burned. I stared out the window, and no one said anything. A few people laughed, not because it was funny, but because laughing was safer.

I didn't cry and I didn't say anything back. I just sat there, willing the ride to end. Everyone filed out like nothing had happened when the bus came to their stop, but Damon's words stayed with me long after the bus pulled away. The uniform I'd resented also protected me, because at least when everyone was dressed the same, I could disappear a little.

Somewhere along the way, I realized I was never going to be that girl, because Lauren was that girl. I began watching from the sidelines instead of joining in.

School dances were a big deal in high school. Both schools had formal dances, and one at the boys' school was coming up. Lauren already had plans to go with her boyfriend. I didn't have a date, but I wanted to go more than I admitted, and the idea of being home while everyone else was there made my stomach sink.

Josh, one of her boyfriend's friends, asked me. I knew he wasn't really interested, and I wasn't either. It felt more like going with a friend without the attraction, which made it easier. We went as part of a group, and that took some of the pressure off. The dance itself was fine, and it wasn't anything memorable. My dress was cuter than the ones I'd worn before, but my mom still had a strong hand in choosing it, like she always did.

My mom cared a lot about how I dressed. Sometimes it felt like she was dressing a much older version of me, someone she wanted me to be rather than the kid I actually was. Lauren's mom was different. She was a busy working mom, rarely around, and didn't seem to care much about what Lauren wore or who she went out with. I noticed the difference even then. Lauren's dresses were always a little sexier, and mine were matronly. I was grateful we wore uniforms to school, because even after Damon's comment, at least the uniform meant everyone blended in, and without it I think I would have felt even more behind Lauren than I already did.

A few months later, Lauren and I fought about something. I don't even remember what. We didn't fight often, so when we did, it usually fizzled out quickly. But then she said it so casually and matter-of-fact. "I had to beg Josh to take you to that dance."

She wasn't angry and it didn't feel like she was being mean. I think that's what hurt the most. She said it as if she was just stating a fact, like of course no one would ask me without her help. I don't remember what I said after that. I just remember my face getting hot and my throat going dry. I had no doubt Josh had laughed about it too, and I figured they all had. I'd spent the whole night being the girl someone got stuck with as a favor.

I started pulling away from Lauren and from the friendships we'd built. I couldn't stand the thought of everyone knowing I was the girl who had to be begged into a date.

I found myself thinking about my mom. She didn't have close female friends either. When she dropped me off at school, she never lingered, and she never got to know the moms at Woodland Heights. She didn't get to know any of my friends' parents. Her world was my dad and her kids, and that was it.

My mom believed real friends were rare and that maybe you'd get a handful at most during your lifetime. At the time, I thought it was sad. Now I wondered if she'd been preparing me.

At some point, I stopped trying so hard. It felt safer to stay on the outside than to keep pressing my face against the glass. If friendships weren't something I could rely on, then I would rely on myself. On the tennis court, at least, I didn't need anyone. No one could leave, and no one could let me down.

It was just me and the game. I told myself that was enough.

Chapter 2: *Playing Alone*

I held my first tennis racquet when I was four or five. By the time I was twelve, I'd spent more hours on the court than I had in my own backyard. My parents invested in private coaches, summer camps, and weekend tournaments. I was good. Good enough that it mattered and quitting wasn't an option. Tennis became the thing I was known for, not the thing I loved. It was THE thing I was good at. And in my family, you didn't waste talent.

I saw the same girls at the club, weekend after weekend. We knew each other's games. We knew which player had a weak backhand or who choked on big points. A few of the girls were friends off the court. But the moment we stepped on opposite sides of the net, friendship stopped mattering. For that match, we were opponents. And I wanted to beat them.

There was one tournament that stuck in my mind - it was the day after Christmas and I was in the sixth grade. Snow was on the ground and my family had packed the car with Christmas presents that needed to be returned to the mall once I played my match or matches depending on whether I advanced. We got to the club and it was full of life. This was a big junior girls' tournament that counted towards USTA rankings. Finding my way to the check-in table, I wasn't nervous. I wasn't excited. I was going through the motions of getting ready to play. Getting my court assignment, I was matched against a top-seeded player. This was going to be hard.

We warmed up. She was a baseline player and her balls were landing deep. Mine were hard but inconsistent. The match started badly and stayed that way. I went down love-three in my first service game after two forehand misses in the net and a double fault. I could already feel my chest tightening.

My strength was power. My weakness was everything that came after the first mistake. I rushed points when I made mistakes. I went for winners too early. When I missed, I missed big. Balls flying straight to the back fence. I could see my mom on the sideline tapping her shoulder, her sign for me to follow through. I slammed my racquet after dumping an easy ball into the net.

Midway through the first set, I chased a short ball wide, slid, and felt something sharp in my ankle. It dulled to a throb but I didn't think anything of it. I kept playing.

I lost the first set quickly. The second wasn't much better. I started playing sloppily. I was late getting to the returns, balls sailing long. The match ended in under an hour.

As I packed my bag, my ankle throbbed. By the time we reached the car, I was limping. In the car, my mom started listing what I'd done wrong. It was a litany of what I should have done differently. I listened without hearing any of it. It was always the same story. Miss. Spiral. Lose.

We made our way to the mall, and I was still hobbling, the limping getting worse. Store after store. "Can we go home? My ankle really hurts."

"We're almost done," my mom said, not slowing down.

I think they thought I was complaining because of my loss. Honestly, my ankle hurt like hell, but I also wanted to get home after losing so quickly. I am a very competitive person and despite how often I practiced, how many camps I attended, how many hours I spent on the court, if I couldn't win in a match, nothing else mattered and I would be pissed.

Our last stop was Macy's, so I found a comfortable chair and put my leg up as my ankle was killing me. My parents were taking a while and the pain was getting worse. I pulled up my pant leg to see if something was wrong, and I was shocked to see that my ankle was huge. It was easily three times its normal size and starting to turn purple.

When my mom emerged from the dressing room, I showed my parents and shock spread across their faces. "Holy shit, you weren't kidding." You could see their expression quickly shift to guilt for ignoring me and making me walk all around the mall. We made a beeline for the car and were on our way to the nearest emergency room. The doctor ordered an x-ray and the result - a fracture along the ankle bone.

Looking back, I must have broken it during the match when I went for that wide ball. I don't know for sure. All I know is I played an entire match on a broken ankle and didn't realize it until we were halfway through the mall.

I chose blue for the color of my cast and then hobbled out of the hospital on crutches, trying not to slip on the ice and snow in the parking lot. One thing that stuck out from this experience is that no one checked in to see how I was while I spent weeks hobbling in a cast and on crutches.

I didn't have teammates to check on me. My coach never called to see how I was. He just continued training his other players and would see me when I was healed. It was just me, my crutches, and the knowledge that I had apparently needed an X-ray to convince my own parents that something was actually wrong.

After my ankle healed, I returned to the court but I never felt that excitement to get back at it. In fact, I'm not sure I ever really liked the game. It was just something that I was good at. Given that it was drilled into us in our family that when you have talent you don't waste it, it's also the reason I was pushed so hard academically too. My parents didn't accept mediocrity and so I continued to thrive in the class and on the court.

When I started high school there was no doubt that I would continue to play tennis. Looking back, I can't remember anyone's name from my high school team, except one, Cheryl, my rival.

Cheryl and I battled for the number one and two spots my junior year. She won. She played number one. I was number two. Our practices were always the two of us, slugging it out. She challenged me to be better because she was better than me. And I hated to admit it.

One practice, we played a challenge match for the top spot. I remember standing on the baseline, watching her serve. It always came in flat and fast. Her mental game was tough. Nothing rattled her. She beat me in straight sets 6-4, 6-4. I was always close, chasing that win, but never quite getting there.

Afterwards, our coach told me I had more power. "You hit harder than she does," he said, like that was supposed to make me feel better. But power didn't matter if I couldn't control it. Cheryl was consistent. Steady. She didn't blow up when she missed. She just kept playing.

I went home that day knowing the truth that she was better than me. And there was nothing I could do about it except keep losing to her in practice and pretending it didn't bother me.

The doubles players had what I didn't, a partner. There was someone to strategize with between points. The pressure to win was shared. They had to learn each other's games, play as a unit. Singles was different. It was just me and whoever stood across the net. And when I lost, there was no one else to blame. When I did play doubles, I played with Cheryl, as the two of us together were unstoppable.

My high school tennis career was unremarkable. I couldn't tell you my record because keeping track of it didn't matter to me anymore or maybe because I didn't want to see how many matches I had actually lost. I received varsity letter recognition all four years, and as my senior year approached, my private coach talked to my parents about my college plans. He said that I was talented enough to play Division I tennis and so I should make recruitment videos and send them to college coaches.

I remember my parents' excitement at this news, probably because that meant scholarship money, and they would get to recoup the costs of all of those years of lessons, camps and hours spent courtside. They wouldn't have to take out loans for my college education.

It turns out I was talented enough for some Division I and II tennis scholarships; however, I made the choice to play at a Division III school and forgo athletic scholarships for academic ones. I didn't want the pressure of Division I sports, and I certainly didn't have the guts to tell my parents I no longer wanted to play tennis. To watch their excitement deflate when I turned down the athletic scholarship offers was painful because it was the first time I saw that disappointment in their eyes. They expected me to have a free or dramatically reduced college education for all of their sacrifices, but I chose me and that didn't sit well with them.

In college, I was one of the top players on the women's team so I played both singles and doubles. But I hit with too much power to practice with my teammates. The only players who could challenge me were on the men's team. So that's where I practiced. Me and the guys. I was the only woman. It left me feeling like an outsider on my own team.

I didn't develop strong friendships with any of my teammates throughout college and was actually grateful that my collegiate tennis career ended my junior year when my knee buckled in the middle of a match.

I was playing in the top doubles spot with my partner Jill. She and I had played together the past few years, so we knew each other's styles well. I hit a backhand down the line and headed to the net. While we were both on the shorter side, we had power and speed so we could stop a lot of shots coming to us at the net. I made it about halfway up the court when all of a sudden I heard a pop sound and ended up on the ground. My right knee had given out. I got up, took a few minutes to move around, and we were able to finish the match. We won easily.

I spent the next hour with the athletic trainer and packs of ice wrapped around my knee. I happened to be heading home to Pittsburgh that weekend for fall break, so I had my parents make me an appointment with an orthopedic doc. My knee was tender that week, sometimes causing me to limp, but I didn't practice so that helped.

The doctor took X-rays and did a physical exam that required him to manipulate my leg around. It hurt like hell. He concluded that my knee didn't track right, something about how I was built.

He suggested surgery but said it wasn't an immediate need. A brace could get me through until then.

When he said surgery wasn't urgent, that I could wait, I felt relief wash over me. I had an out. A legitimate reason to stop playing without admitting I wanted to quit. I never scheduled the surgery during my junior year. I told people I was injured, recovering, waiting for the right time. I didn't play my senior year. Looking back, I was done. I just couldn't say it out loud.

A week after graduating from college, I finally had knee surgery.

It's been over two decades since I played competitive tennis. I don't know if the sport taught me resilience or just how to be alone. I had no one to turn to between points. No one to look at when I was down and say we got this. How to keep going even when no one was watching. But maybe that's the same thing.

I learned to be alone on the court. Even in doubles, I never got close to any of my partners, not because I didn't want to, but because I didn't know how when our partnership was primarily about winning. And I was about to learn how to be alone everywhere else too.

Chapter 3: *When She Chose Him*

It was the fall of my junior year of high school. Lauren and I went to one of the school dances in the gym. We didn't drive together. Back when things weren't strained between us, you could bet that one of our parents would have driven us into the city for a dance and picked us up after to drive us home. Lauren was dating a new guy, Joe, a star forward on the soccer team. She arrived with Joe and his friends and my parents drove me since I didn't have my license yet.

This particular dance was one that is seared in my memory because it forever changed things between me and Lauren. The gym's lights were dimmed low, the air stale and filled with the overwhelming scent of Cool Water cologne. The DJ bounced between 90s R&B slow songs and grunge, the bass vibrating through the bleachers.

I hovered at the edge of the popular crowd, close enough to belong but never fully settled. I'd gone to grade school with many of them and I was Lauren's friend from home, which meant I was included by proximity.

I was dancing with Sean, one of the most popular seniors at the boys' school. We always found our way to each other at dances, always friendly at football games and parties, familiar without ever being close. By then our dancing followed a predictable rhythm. Him always stepping behind me, his hands on my hips, us grinding to the music. It was thrilling and terrifying all at once, suddenly aware of your body, all those eyes watching.

Rob Base's *It Takes Two To Make A Thing Go Right* was playing when something shifted. Out of the corner of my eye, I caught Lauren and Joe, faces tight, yelling at each other near the edge of the gym. Even over the music, I could feel the intensity of it all. My stomach dropped before my mind could catch up. I knew Joe drank a lot, and I had a gut feeling he was drunk again. I looked at Sean and something passed between us, knowing that whatever was happening over there wasn't good at all.

"I have to go see if she's okay." Sean looked concerned. "He's a dick when he's drinking. I am coming with you." By the time we got over to Lauren, a crowd was forming. No one knew quite what to do. Joe was animated, arms flailing. Was he going to hit her?

I'd heard rumors that he got physical with her when he was drunk. She'd never said it outright, but I had my suspicions. The volume between them grew. Some of Joe's friends tried to pull him back. He shrugged them off.

Without thinking, I stepped between them.

I saw what looked like Joe raising his fist. Was he actually going to hit her in public? Was I imagining it? Was he just waving his arms to make a point? I couldn't be sure. But I wasn't just going to stand there and do nothing.

What was he going to do, hit me? Maybe. But I wasn't thinking clearly. I think I yelled at him to back the fuck up. Or maybe I just thought about it. Either way, I was standing there not backing down. Joe may have been popular, a star soccer player, but he was an asshole to the core.

I grabbed Lauren and pulled her away. She was shaking, cheeks red, eyes wet. She was clearly embarrassed and scared.

"What the hell was that about?" My voice was sharper than it needed to be.

"Nothing. He's not a bad guy. He just had a little too much to drink tonight."

"Did he drive you here like this?"

"No, Rob drove us. He's the DD tonight."

"You can do better than him. He's such an ass. Why are you wasting your time on him? You can have anyone you want."

"You wouldn't understand. You've never even had a boyfriend."

"Like that matters. I'm not going to stand there and watch you be treated this way, not by him, not by anyone. This isn't like you."

She didn't argue. She didn't explain. After a moment, she left me standing there and walked back toward him, already smoothing things over, already ignoring the warning signs and choosing toxic over being alone.

She chose him. We walked away from each other at that moment, the space between us widening with every step. We never found our way back. At the time, I wouldn't let myself believe that neither one of us would fight for our friendship. I thought once she broke up with Joe and had some time to realize what a douche he was, that we would begin to rebuild our relationship.

But as time passed, reality sunk in. It was happening again. We never talked about that night again. We just slowly stopped calling each other. I started to ride to school with Amy, a friend from my hometown, instead. Her dad drove us because neither of us had our licenses. I saw Lauren around school and the neighborhood. We exchanged pleasantries but nothing beyond that.

Just like at the pool when I was younger, just like when Josh had to be begged to take me to a dance, I was on the outside again, but this time, I'd chosen it. This time I'd stepped between Lauren and Joe, standing up for her, and she picked him anyway.

Being an extrovert, I put a brave face on and found a new group of girls to hang out with, but again, never quite fitting in. I pretended that I was better off with guys as friends. They certainly would never hurt me like any girl would.

But I didn't fight for Lauren either.

I decided it was all about Joe. She chose him over me, case closed. But in reality, I don't know if I would have fought for her even if he wasn't in the picture. Our friendship had been fracturing long before he showed up. The dance with Josh. The feeling that I was always half a step behind. The certainty that I wasn't really hers the way she was mine.

Maybe Joe was just my easy way out. Maybe it was less painful to let her go than to admit I'd never felt as secure in our friendship as I wanted to.

If girls were going to leave anyway, at least with guys, I knew the rules. Guys are easier. Or so I thought.

Part Two:

Losing Myself

Chapter 4: *Settling for Less*

College was supposed to be a fresh start. I went to a Catholic school in Washington, DC, living in a co-ed dorm. My roommate and I were polar opposites. I was on the tennis team, had Andre Agassi posters on my wall, and could talk to anyone. She was more shy and loved to dance. We got along well, and I liked her. But we were different in every way.

All of the girls on our floor seemed to click with someone right away. Groups formed fast, tight little circles, and I wasn't in any of them. I ended up finding my best friend in a guy from the dorm next door, Drew.

I spent most of my time in his room, probably driving his roommate crazy with my constant presence. Thursday nights were sacred. It was our non-negotiable time to watch ER. It didn't take long before I developed a crush on Drew.

And I watched from the sidelines as he fawned over one of the girls in my dorm, someone I actually became close with. She was on her way to becoming a really close friend. Of course you can guess what happened. They hooked up during our freshman year. Once again, I was on the sidelines, watching my crush and my new friend together.

Thankfully, it didn't last long. I felt a small, guilty pleasure when she tossed him aside. But it didn't erase the hurt. She'd known I liked him when it happened.

I had a few crushes my first few years, some more promising than others, but they all ended the same way. I was always left wondering what was wrong with me.

Drew and my friendship grew over the years. We had shared experiences as student athletes and being RAs. During the summers we wrote letters to each other, because while email was around, there was nothing like old-fashioned pen and paper. Our friendship always had some flirtatious banter but it wasn't until our junior year that we drifted into a friends with benefits situation.

We settled into the insecure rhythm of young adults fooling around without admitting feelings. We teetered on the line between friendship and something more but never crossing into something formally defined. I frequently told myself this was enough. I didn't need a title to define what this was. But that story was getting old. I did want to admit my feelings and I felt like maybe this wasn't just all feeling on my part. I was going to ask for what I wanted.

It was one of our Thursday nights, ER on the TV. I was nervous, palms sweating. We always watched in my room because I was the one with the TV. I planned to bring up the "what are we doing" question once we finished watching. As the credits rolled, I chickened out but found myself quickly relieved, because Drew immediately started talking about Maria, a new crush he had. He couldn't stop talking about her. I had my answer. He didn't feel the same, and I would not risk a friendship over feelings. So I stayed quiet.

The benefits aspect of our friendship fizzled, and by the time college ended, things had gone back to how they started. We were just friends. I learned a big lesson from my time with Drew. I was willing to accept less than I wanted because it was safer to keep my feelings hidden. I convinced myself that what I imagined in my head was enough, even when it wasn't. Drew and I stayed friends after graduation. We'd text occasionally, see each other when life wasn't too busy. Our friendship remained strong, unwavering. And I accepted it.

Somehow, after all of this, I still believed guy friendships were easier. They were less complicated. Or at least they felt that way when I convinced myself I was getting the best of both worlds.

I established myself as one of the guys early on. They didn't hold grudges the way girls did. There was no dissecting every word you said. You could hang out, talk about nothing, and it was enough. No one was keeping score.

When I moved to Italy for graduate school, I found myself living in an apartment with 14 guys. There was an opening at one point to join an apartment of 9 women, and when the landlord asked if I wanted to switch apartments, I emphatically said no thanks.

I was sharing a bathroom with a guy who washed his bath towel so infrequently that it was stiff and smelled like mildew. The drying racks in the living room were always filled with boxers and athletic socks. The kitchen trash became a competitive sport, everyone adding just one more thing, daring gravity, until someone's empty beer bottle finally took the whole thing down. Nobody ever volunteered to empty it. And the one to make it topple was the one who had to take it out.

I was 23 and living in Rome, and I had never felt more at home.

In law school, I was friendly with a few girls, but I really connected with the guys in my class. I just naturally felt more comfortable joking around with them. I could be crass. I could offer advice on girls. I could hang out at the bar and wasn't a lightweight. I could dissect the Steelers game. But what I couldn't do was stay connected with the women in my class.

This continued as I established my life in DC. I would spend my Sundays at the bar watching football all day. I would go to the strip club for lunch with my guy coworkers and then we would grab a beer after work for happy hours. I played on their kickball and softball teams. I sometimes laughed at jokes about women because it was safer to see myself as one of the guys than to be vulnerable and embrace my feminine side. That opened me up to rejection and who wants that.

I noticed the dynamic change as my friends entered serious relationships and marriages. The wives didn't want me around, especially when there was history with their husbands. At the time, I didn't fully understand it, but now I do. I used to believe being friends with exes or guys you've fooled around with was a sign of emotional maturity. What I see now is that it isn't always healthy. History doesn't disappear just because people decide to call it friendship. Boundaries have to be clear. Feelings have to be honest. Respect has to come first. Those were lessons I wasn't mature enough to understand in my 20s and 30s, but ones that grew with time and experience.

My friendships with men taught me a lot over the years, especially about what I wanted in a partner and a husband. But knowing that didn't mean I knew how to pick one.

My 20s and early 30s were a disaster when it came to men. I bounced from one bad relationship to another, convinced each time that this one would be different. They weren't. My dating history reads like a cautionary tale, or maybe a comedy, depending on your sense of humor. Either way, I spent those years proving to myself that I wasn't sure how to pick the right guy and that being alone often felt worse than being with someone who didn't see me.

It started with Mark. We'd known each other in undergrad but reconnected right before I started law school. What began as friendship turned into long-distance dating. For the next three years, we traveled twice a month to see each other. We vacationed with each other's families. We talked about marriage. On paper, he was everything I thought I wanted. Smart, kind, good looking, from a wonderful family.

But there was one nagging problem. Sex. Or rather, the lack of it.

He wasn't ready. He told me it was his faith, Catholic guilt. I understood because I'd grown up with the same conditioning. I could wait. It would be worth it. Waiting was what good Catholic girls did.

But the waiting turned me inside out. I felt undesirable. Unwanted. Like there was something wrong with me that made him not want me that way. I remember the weekend that changed everything for me. A mutual college friend was getting married in Charleston, SC, and we were going to the wedding.

Mark and I had taken a few trips over the years, but this one felt different. I was getting ready to graduate from law school and move to be closer to him. This felt like a possible preview for our future. I was hoping for this to be a shifting moment in our relationship. The stresses of school were nearly behind me. Our future was clear as our long-distance back-and-forth was coming to a close. We would be alone this weekend, knowing we were among the very small handful of friends invited.

The wedding was held outdoors, a romantic setting among shady, moss-laden oak trees and a lagoon filled with swans. It was early May so the weather wasn't too humid. I was wearing a strapless black knee-length dress. Mark wore a navy blue suit. We looked so good together. But looking good together wasn't enough.

As the bride and groom were saying their vows, hand in hand, I closed my eyes trying to imagine that it was me and Mark up there. And I couldn't do it. I desperately tried, but I just couldn't imagine us up there, saying "I do" to each other. I thought this was what I wanted, and now I couldn't imagine marrying him.

The reception was lovely but I was more anxious about what would happen when we got back to the hotel. I was hoping this would finally be the time he would let go. It was just us, alone in a beautiful hotel, surrounded by love and wedding bliss. I remember straddling him, trying one more time, but he put his hand to my chest and said that he still wasn't ready. I'd never felt more rejected in my life.

I went to the bathroom, filled the tub with warm water, and tried to forget the sting of that rejection. My boyfriend, after three years and professing our love for each other, still couldn't sleep with me. I sat in that tub wondering what was wrong with me. Why wasn't I enough?

My frustration curdled into resentment. I was angry all the time. I was pissed at him for not wanting me and at myself for staying. Right before graduation, Matt and Kyle, two of my close guy friends from school, told me I deserved better than Mark. They knew I was moving to DC to be near him but they also knew me. They had seen my spark fizzle over these past three years and they called me on it.

Graduation weekend, Mark said he had a gift in the car. While he went to get it, I sat there thinking that this is it. This is the proposal. We'd been together for three years. Everyone expected it. I expected it even though I was secretly hoping it wasn't happening.

He came back with a fancy espresso machine. Practical. Maybe even thoughtful since he knew I missed Italy so much. But not a ring. I ended it the next day. He was shocked. I wasn't. I'd been ending it in my head for months.

The night I arrived in DC to start my new life, Amy and I went to a bar to celebrate my graduation. She told me we were meeting up with some of her work friends and that's the night I met Noah. He was black, funny, smart, and the chemistry was immediate.

He sat down next to me and we started talking about sports. He didn't quiz me or act surprised that I had opinions. We just talked, and at some point I noticed I'd angled my whole body toward him and forgot that we were there with other people.

We met after work for baseball games, and happy hours turned into dinners. He cooked for me when I was swamped with work and studying for the Bar exam. He'd run me a bath in his apartment after long days. He even went furniture shopping to help me outfit my new apartment. We laughed, something I felt like I hadn't really done in years. We found comfort in each other's presence. I wondered if it was dating or just deep friendship, and I didn't ask. He was my escape from the chaos of life at that time.

We spent nearly a year together like this, never quite defining our status, but making the time for each other. I thought maybe this is what it's supposed to feel like since Mark and I had talked about our future but we never moved forward.

My parents met him once, but only as my friend. Noah was black and that was something my parents wouldn't have been thrilled about. When my mom met him, she pulled me aside and told me she knew we were more than friends and to have fun, but don't get serious and don't ever tell my father the truth. I was an adult and still calibrating my life around what would or wouldn't be acceptable to them.

Noah and I went out one Friday and he came back to my place after. We were sitting on the couch when he got a serious look on his face.

"I have had so much fun hanging out with you, but this isn't working."

"Um…okay?" Trying to keep a straight face, I sat in silence until he continued.

"It's me. It's not you. I just don't want anything serious right now," he said, fidgeting with his hands. "But I still want to be friends. I have fun hanging out with you. I just don't want a relationship now."

"Friends. Yeah, of course we can be friends." I would not let him see me cry.

"Okay, well I should be going."

He hugged me goodbye and I was left feeling duped. How could I have misread everything? Or did I? We never talked about our feelings towards each other and the word love never came up. Maybe I just made this all bigger in my head.

Unfortunately things continued to stay confusing. We were still in the same social circle and every time a group of us hung out, there were stolen glances, secret hand holding and continued flirting. We drifted into each other's beds a few more times over the years but it went no further.

One of the most hurtful parts of my time with Noah was that, several years after we were last together, he texted to say he had a gift for me. He was traveling and had to buy it for me because it was from a place we had discussed years before. A man still thinking of me but not choosing me. By then, I knew the script well enough to recognize the hope rising before I could stop it.

When Noah told me he didn't want a relationship, I was crushed. It was Mark all over again. Although it was for different reasons, the result was the same. I wasn't the girl men wanted.

I had moved on after Mark, but he stayed stuck. After a brutal two days of taking the Bar exam, I was waiting on the train platform in Baltimore to head back to DC and there he was. He guessed at what time my exam would end and that I would need to catch the train back to DC, so he showed up on the platform and waited. Months after we had broken up. I had no words. He handed me a letter and professed his love. He begged me to take him back. I was so angry he chose this moment to fight for me. After all those years together, knowing what I wanted, needed. I told him to go home. I read the letter on the train. He poured his heart out and said all the things that girls want to hear. But it didn't matter. I couldn't go back. I knew then that I had made the right choice months earlier. For the first time, I understood that wanting to be wanted wasn't the same as needing to stay in a relationship that didn't fit.

After Mark and Noah, I didn't suddenly get better at choosing men. If anything, I got worse.

These years blurred into a series of almosts and not-quites. I had a few short relationships and all of them were bad fits. Men who wanted pieces of me but not the responsibility of me. Each time, I believed this one would be different but it never was. Being alone still felt more frightening than being disappointed, so I stayed longer than I should have, ignored what I knew, and kept hoping something would eventually stick.

When I first moved back to DC, I was working at a law firm, shadowing a senior attorney. He was in his 40s, married with two kids, and someone positioned as a mentor. It was January, so I had only been working there for about eight months and I was shadowing him for a personal injury trial in DC. The weather wasn't cooperating and our trial kept getting delayed. After what should have been a two-day trial max, this stretched over a few weeks.

The jury got past the delays and everyone just wanted this trial to be over. It was a Friday afternoon and we received a settlement offer but it wasn't even close to the six figures in damages we were seeking. My mentor immediately suggested our client decline the offer. He was convinced the jury would award her more. Our client paused, looked at me, and then asked for my opinion. I was scared because what the hell did I know? I had been an attorney for mere months. I followed my gut and I told her to take the offer. My mentor gave me a pained look.

She ultimately took his advice and left it in the jury's hands. Their deliberation was less than an hour. Five thousand dollars was all they awarded. In personal injury cases, the clients don't pay attorneys' fees upfront. If there's an award, the firm usually takes around 30%, with the hopes of recouping costs and having extra for profits. This was a total loss for our client and for the firm. He was pissed and wanted to blow off steam.

After the judge dismissed everyone in the courtroom, my mentor asked if I would join him for a drink with another judge, not the one from our case. We had a drink in the judge's chambers and then left the courthouse. We passed a bar on the way to the subway, and he wanted to stop for another drink. This was a really big loss for the firm and he wasn't happy.

I didn't think anything of it, because it seemed like normal behavior in DC. Coworkers having a few drinks after work. Bars were filled with suits after five. One drink turned into many. Somewhere in the middle of that night, he had me pinned against a wall, his hand groping my breasts, his mouth on mine. I remember kissing him back before the fog cut and I finally said no. I remember insisting I was leaving. I remember being at the base of the subway stairs. Then nothing. I woke up the next morning in my own bed, alone, fully clothed, with no memory of how I got home.

I'd been drunk before but I'd never lost time like that. To this day, I have always wondered if there was something in my drink. All I know is that I got home safe, and I have no idea how. That terrifies me even now.

When I went back to work on Monday, we both acted as if nothing had happened. It made me wonder whether I had imagined the whole thing with how nonchalant he was behaving. Later that week, we were in a courthouse hallway. He ran into another lawyer and went to introduce me. He paused, his face blank. It seemed as though he couldn't remember my name.

"Hi, my name is Chrissy," I said as I extended a handshake.

When the other lawyer walked away, he looked at me and said, "See, if you would have fucked me, I would have remembered your name." That sentence landed harder than the night itself.

I reported what happened to one of the women I trusted in the firm. I was humiliated and felt like it was my fault. I begged her to keep it quiet. The firm moved our offices farther apart and I was assigned to shadow someone new. Everyone went back to work like nothing happened.

I stayed long enough to find another job. Then I left law entirely.

By my late 20s, something had settled into me. I started to believe that I was good enough to want, but never good enough to keep. Sex replaced meaningful connection. I let attention stand in for care. Every time a man desired me, it quieted the old voice that told me I wasn't pretty enough, chosen enough. It never stayed quiet for long.

Years later, when my dad died, I got a letter in the mail. A handwritten note from Drew, like all the letters we used to write when we were in college.

> *Dear Chrissy,*
>
> *I can't imagine what you're going through and I just wanted you to know I am thinking of you. You've been so brave and strong for your family these past couple of months. I am proud of you. It takes a strong woman to do what you've done. I'm sure it's a difficult time for you and your family and I want you to know I am always here for you.*
>
> *Thanks for all you've done for me. I think about you often. I'm so sorry for your loss.*
>
> *Love you.*
>
> *-Drew*

I sat there holding that letter for a long time. He wasn't able to make it to the funeral but when I called him after, we talked for a while. It was easy, the way it had always been with Drew.

In college, I'd wanted something from him he couldn't give me. I'd convinced myself that what we had as friends with benefits was enough, even when it wasn't. I'd been scared to ask for more and relieved when I didn't have to.

But this, what we have now, is better than anything I thought I wanted back then.

We were what we were when we needed each other in that way. But as we both grew up and experienced life, we found our way to something real. A lasting, loving friendship. No confusion or games. Neither of us wondering if the other felt more.

It doesn't look like what I once thought it would. But somehow it ended up better.

I never considered myself someone who slept around. But looking back at some of the situations I put myself in, I cringe. I mistook access for intimacy. I handed over power and called it being laid-back. I made myself believe I was fine when I wasn't. I wanted one of these stories to finally end differently.

It didn't. And when I met Ryan, I learned the difference between desperate and dangerous.

Chapter 5: *Surviving Him*

I met Ryan when I was 29. We started talking one night during happy hour at a bar near my apartment. I don't remember how it started, only that it did. Before we left, he said we should hang out sometime. Not go on a date, hang out. That distinction matters now. He was clear from the beginning. I was the one who turned it into something else in my head.

The first time we got together we went bowling or something like that. I don't even remember the details, which probably says enough. What I do remember is the way the night ended. He'd had a few beers. He walked me to my car, and before I got in, he turned and pissed in the parking lot.

I stood there watching him, thinking, *what the fuck are you doing?* I remember knowing, right then, that I should get in my car and never see him again.

Then he kissed me.

And I did what I had learned to do. I minimized it. I explained it away. I needed to believe it wasn't that big of a deal. I said I'd see him again.

I don't remember how Ryan and I slid into what we became. I only remember a pull. I wanted to be around him in a way that didn't make sense, even to me. He was nothing like the men I had been with before. He was vulgar and abrasive. He moved through the world like rules were for other people. And for reasons I still don't fully understand, I was all in.

I spent years with him and never once felt loved. Not really. I didn't feel cherished or even particularly wanted. I was anxious, always on alert. Grateful when he was kind but desperate not to set him off.

At first, it was small things. I lent him money, a little here and a little there. Something always came up and I fell for whatever lie he dished out. He still owes me four thousand dollars. I also frequently let him use my car because I took the subway to work. He hit something in a parking lot and never dealt with it, so when my lease ended, the bill landed on me.

Our apartments were within walking distance of each other. I had a perfectly good one-bedroom apartment and he had a two-bedroom with a roommate. His roommate was older and mostly kept to himself. It was a typical bachelor apartment. Clothes flung over the kitchen chairs, remote controls and video game covers on the ottoman, dishes in the kitchen sink, and a bathroom that wasn't always clean. It felt like I was back in my apartment in Rome with all of those guys, except now I was almost 30, not fresh out of college. Ryan kept his mattress on the floor, and somehow, I was always the one leaving my place to sleep there.

There were signs I ignored because it felt easier to believe him than myself. Once I found a used condom in his bathroom. I came flying out of there yelling that he was cheating. He quickly denied it and said it was his roommate's. His roommate, who constantly talked about never getting laid. I knew it was a lie and I stayed.

Ryan had a serious girlfriend years before. They, like me and Mark, had talked about marriage. The difference between us was that I had long since moved on from my former relationship, but not Ryan. He talked about his ex like she was a ghost that still lived in the room. He made it clear I wasn't her. Would never be her. I absorbed that as fact. And I stayed.

Sex was a part of the relationship but it was unpredictable. Sometimes I felt like we were on good footing and that we had a normal adult sex life. Other times, I was made to feel like I had to earn it or negotiate for it. I accepted that wanting him meant wanting whatever scraps he gave. What the fuck!

We had been together for about a year and a half when I first experienced Ryan's dangerous wrath. We were going to Pittsburgh for the weekend to visit my family. It was rush hour on a Friday night, the worst time you could try to leave the city, but we both worked late that day, so we knew it would take us longer to make the trip.

We were 20 minutes into our drive, him driving my car, when I called my mom to tell her we were on our way and that it would be late when we got in so if they needed to head to bed, I would lock up the house and see them in the morning. I remember setting the phone in between my legs. A few minutes later, I said something that pissed Ryan off. For the life of me, I can't remember what it was, but it really doesn't matter. He was yelling at me, raising his right hand in the air. I didn't think he was going to hit me, but maybe I was just telling myself that to calm my nerves. My first instinct when someone picks a fight with me is to fight back. And that's what I did. I started yelling back at him. Thankfully traffic was stopped, so at least we weren't flying down the highway like this.

"Chrissy, are you okay? Chrissy! Tell me you're okay!" My mom's frantic voice filled the car.

I had somehow accidentally called her while the phone was in between my legs. She'd heard everything. I was mortified and even angrier that Ryan put me in this situation.

I tried to calm my mom down and told her it was nothing. She wasn't convinced. I reminded her of our ETA and hung up. Ryan and I sat in silence for the whole drive. My mind was racing but at no point did I think I needed to leave this relationship.

That weekend was excruciating. My parents tried to talk to me when Ryan wasn't around. They told me they didn't like him. I shut it down. Their disapproval almost made me hold on tighter.

If they were right, then I had made another wrong choice. And I couldn't stand that.

Little by little, I disappeared from my friendships. Sarah. Amy. They had husbands and babies. Our lives had shifted in different directions. In reality, I didn't want anyone to see me like this. I wasn't sure how to explain why I couldn't leave.

I stopped letting people see the real me. Not because they wouldn't have cared, but because caring would have required answers I didn't have the strength to give. The smaller my circle became, the easier it was to pretend everything was fine. Silence became part of the routine.

Ryan and I spent every day together for years. Approaching our second year together, we decided to spend Thanksgiving in Florida with his family. My parents were pissed about this, but I didn't care. Admitting they were right wasn't an option. Things between me and Ryan had been good for a while so I wasn't worried about this trip.

We boarded our flight from DC and Ryan was sweet, holding my hand on the plane. I was taking the scraps of affection and justifying away the moments when I felt like discarded trash.

Before we left I had told Ryan I wanted to get together with one of my closest friends from college since he was living near Ryan's family. Drew had been in Florida for a few years for grad school and when I reached out to make plans, he was all in. We grabbed a quick lunch with Drew when we landed.

Two minutes after we said our goodbyes, I got a text: *He's an asshole. What are you doing with this guy?*

I sat in the car fighting back tears. One of the people who knew me better than anyone called me out, and I knew he was right. But I also felt sad for another reason. Drew never wanted me and was that part of the reason I let myself get into this situation?

Meeting Ryan's family was eye opening. To say they were rough around the edges was an understatement. They had a bite to them, much like Ryan. We had taken his mom with us as we were running errands one afternoon and she and Ryan got into a screaming fight in the car. I was so uncomfortable. I had definitely had my fair share of moments with my parents, but this was next level. When it ended, she turned to me and said, casually, "This is why I used to beat him as a child." I remember staring out the window and thinking, *Of course this is where he learned it.*

A few weeks later, while back home in DC, we took a late-night run to the grocery store to grab dinner. We got back to the car and once again started fighting. He took his set of my car keys, threw them under the car, and walked away. Of course I didn't have my keys on me at the time. It was December and very dark outside. Standing there stunned, I was willing myself not to cry. I took out my phone flashlight and crawled on my hands and knees around the car to see if I could find my keys. A woman watched this whole encounter and came up to me after he stormed off. She asked if I was okay. I nodded, fighting back tears.

"You deserve better, sweetheart," she said gently. A stranger called me out.

After finally finding my car keys, I drove home numb. And I stayed.

We were on good footing for a few months after this and I wanted to get away. It was a long winter and the beach was calling my name. I asked Ryan if he'd want to do a trip to the Caribbean for a four-day getaway. He was all in. This was going to be good for us, I thought.

As the trip approached, he started complaining the entire time about work, about money, about me. He was self-employed and said I was costing him money by making him be there. I asked several times if he wanted to cancel. He always said no. So we went and it was miserable. We were in a romantic adults-only resort, and he spent the majority of the time moping about how he didn't want to be there.

I should have known to avoid trips with him after this, but when he asked me to join him and a few friends in Vegas for the weekend, I said yes. He and four friends were flying out on a Wednesday and I was going to join them on Friday. Forty-eight hours in Vegas with five guys. What could go wrong?

When my flight landed, I took a cab to the hotel where I found the guys in the pool, beers in hand, and several hours ahead of me drinking. I dropped my bags off in the room and joined them in the pool. Drinking all afternoon poolside should have been my warning sign for what was to come, but was it? Nope.

We all shared a suite at the Venetian, Ryan and I getting the room with the king bed. When I first arrived he was sweet and affectionate, which wasn't common in front of his friends. For once I was being treated like a girl, not just one of the guys.

Saturday night we had dinner reservations at a steakhouse and then off to a club where they paid for a booth. I was getting ready in the bathroom when Ryan walked in. He had this possessive look in his eyes, one that I rarely saw from him. He started kissing me passionately. Hands roaming. He pushed up the hem of my dress and took me against the bathroom counter. I ended up with a massive black and purple bruise covering half of the back of my leg. He took it as a badge of honor, because "he had fucked me good," he said proudly. I was in pain, barely able to sit comfortably.

Later that night, after dinner and the club, we were all getting ready to leave to head back to the hotel when I heard Ryan yelling. I walked back to where he was and I saw him engaged in a screaming match with what looked to be a mother and daughter. What the fuck was happening? His friends tried to coax him away and he wasn't budging. I tried to touch his arm to say let this go. He gave me a death stare and didn't move. His friends and I walked away.

As we were in this long hotel hallway, I heard him yell my name. His best friend was standing next to me and we both turned around. Ryan threw a can of Coke at my head. He missed my face by inches. His best friend told me to pack my bags and that he would catch a flight with me that night.

I didn't take his friend up on the offer. I told him I would be fine to catch my 6:00am flight the next morning. I was leaving before they were so I could handle a few more hours before I needed to head to the airport. Flying home with his friend would have made things worse and I was too afraid to do anything but stay.

I excused his behavior on this trip to being drunk in Vegas. And I stayed. As the months passed, we were growing further apart. We weren't fighting as much. It was just a quiet distance. Until it wasn't quiet.

One night we walked from my apartment to his and we started arguing. For the life of me, I don't remember what about. And then all I remember is that once we got into his building, his hands were around my neck, squeezing my throat. He held me off the ground by my neck while continuing to yell in my face. All I can recall is him telling me not to ever say or do whatever it was again. Once he felt like his message was delivered, he stormed off to the elevator, leaving me gasping for air. Stunned. Terrified.

A man from his apartment building was in the mailroom and saw everything. When Ryan was gone, he came over to me, shaken. "Are you okay? Do you need help right now? Do you want to call the police?"

I couldn't speak. I told him I was fine. I wasn't fine. I walked out of the building and went home. That wasn't the first time someone offered help. It was just the last time before I finally stopped pretending this was normal.

We broke up not long after that, and I became a shell of myself. I didn't recognize myself anymore.

When I finally ended things, I knew I needed help. I had to understand how I'd gotten myself into that situation and why I'd stayed for three years. It felt like waking up from a nightmare only to look in the mirror and not know the person who was staring back.

I found a therapist near my apartment. He was an older man, late fifties, gray curly hair, and glasses. He wore Brooks Brothers button-downs and khakis. His office was painted beige and of course there was the required therapist's couch and end table with a box of tissues. The whole setup looked like I had imagined a therapist's office would.

My first session was unremarkable. By the second and third, I was holding onto that tissue box like a lifeline. For two sessions straight, I just cried.

And then I stopped going.

I'm not sure if it was because I didn't feel connected to him or because once I'd had a few good cries, I reverted to what I knew. I'd let myself fall apart just enough to feel like I'd done something about it. Then I picked myself back up, shoved all the feelings down, and moved on.

Looking back, that's exactly the problem. I treated therapy the same way I treated grief. Get in, get out, and don't let it go too deep.

I didn't really heal before I met Jeff.

About two months after I left Ryan, I was heading to the subway on my way to work and Jeff had just come up the steps heading to his job. We passed each other, kept walking, then both turned around at the same time. We held smiles for longer than normal. It felt like something out of a movie.

That night, I was walking Scooby around the block. In our neighborhood, everyone knew me and my dog. As we passed the contracting company on the corner, the guy from that morning was standing in the doorway. We recognized each other immediately. He introduced himself as Jeff and nodded to the man next to him. "This is Miguel."

We talked for a few minutes. Then they invited me to happy hour across the street. I said thanks, maybe another time. My confidence was wrecked after Ryan. I wasn't in a place to even think about men.

So of course, I took Scooby home, paced my apartment, and argued with myself for 20 minutes. Then I put on concealer and lip gloss and walked back out the door.

I went to the bar, nervous as hell. What was I doing? I saw Jeff and Miguel at the bar and walked over. They were shocked to see me but then immediately both gave me hugs. They were happy

I was there. Jeff and Miguel were not only co-workers but best friends. The three of us ended up talking for hours. When they asked if I was single, the subject of Ryan came up. They knew him. He was friends with the company's owner. We spent an absurd amount of time talking about what a douche he was. They barely knew him, but they hated him on my behalf. And that felt good.

As I was getting ready to leave, Jeff touched my arm. "Would you like to go to dinner this weekend?"

"A date?" I wasn't ready. But this felt different.

"Yes, a date." I saw Miguel out of the corner of my eye, a disappointed look on his face.

"Let's do it." As I walked home, I let my excitement overshadow any rational thought telling me I was in no place to start dating someone yet.

Jeff and I didn't really make sense on paper. I'd gone to law school; he worked with his hands. I wore suits to the office. He hadn't gone to college. He had kids, and I was convinced I never wanted any. It should have mattered more than it did. With him, things were easy. We laughed a lot and I needed to laugh after the last three years with Ryan.

After a few weeks together, Jeff told me he was falling in love with me, and because I wanted that to be true, I believed him.

One weekend, he went out of town with friends but he promised he would meet me Sunday afternoon for a friend's kid's birthday party. Sunday morning came and I hadn't heard from him. His phone went straight to voicemail. I called a few times and left one message. The party came and went. He didn't show. By early evening, I still hadn't heard anything and called Miguel. I thought something bad had happened. He hadn't heard from him either. Much later, Miguel told me the truth. Jeff had been with another girl. I was stunned. It was happening again. He cheated on me like Ryan did.

The next day when Jeff and I had the chance to talk, he broke things off. My repeated calling, he said, meant I was crazy. I was crushed.

So I did the thing that had probably made me sound crazy. I fucked Miguel.

I think I believed that being desired sexually was being seen. That it gave me power. But in reality, I was giving away all my power by settling for anything less than what I deserved.

The guys I'd been with were from different backgrounds, different races, different education levels. I didn't have a type. A friend once called me the "United Nations of dating." What I really was? Desperate. Desperate for validation. I needed for one of these relationships to finally stick.

If I couldn't make it work with Mark, the guy who on paper was everything I should have wanted, then where was I going to find love?

About six months after things ended with Jeff, my dad was diagnosed with cancer. My focus shifted entirely to my family. Later, after he died, my mom told me something he'd said to her during one of their quiet moments when he was sick. "God, I hope Chrissy doesn't marry an asshole one day."

The last guy I'd brought home was Ryan. No wonder he was worried.

One thing I had to admit was that I didn't have close girlfriends that I confided in about how I was really feeling. Sure, before Sarah and Amy got married, I shared stories of my frustrations or sexual escapades, but to truly let them in, see the insecurities that surrounded my relationships with these men, that I didn't do. I was denying it to myself. I had a great career. I was successful, outgoing, and had a wide social circle. But deep down, not many knew the real me. And when I was at my lowest, I pushed the women away out of fear of embarrassment and jealousy for the lives they had that I so desperately wanted.

What I learned from Ryan was how to survive. How to keep going no matter what. After him, I felt unbreakable.

But I wasn't learning resilience. I was learning how to perform strength when everything inside me was breaking.

And I was about to get a lot of practice.

Chapter 6: *Breaking Wasn't an Option*

I remember the first time I saw a dead body. I was 12 and it was my Grandpa Joe. He was my dad's dad.

Most of my memories of my grandfather are faded now, but I do remember a few things…like his hands. He had calloused palms and his fingers rested in an almost bent position. He was an Italian immigrant who never went to school beyond the eighth grade. He spent 63 years as a shoemaker in my hometown. I can still smell the leather and glue when I think about his tiny shop.

When he wasn't working, he was tending to his garden in the backyard. Growing and sharing the perfect tomato was his love language. My grandmother was a master in the kitchen so the fruits of his backyard labor always made their way into some delicious dish devoured during our large and loud Sunday family dinners.

At 83 my grandfather was diagnosed with pancreatic cancer. He underwent a massive surgery within a week of his diagnosis and he died a few days later. A pulmonary embolism killed him two days before he was supposed to come home. I was beyond devastated. I could call my grandfather at 9pm on a Friday night telling him I was craving homemade pasta and within 30 minutes he would be at our door with a piping hot dish and homemade bread on the side. It didn't seem real.

Italians in my hometown treated funeral homes like a ritual. Women in black dresses, men in three-piece suits, whether they knew the deceased or not, they would sit in the funeral home for hours. I'd never been to one before my grandfather died.

I wrote a letter to my grandfather to tell him all of the things I was going to miss about him. I had it folded in my hand as I stood in the funeral home hallway. My parents were already in the viewing room and I was dreading walking in there. I had never seen a dead body before and now I was going to see one of my favorite people lying in a casket. My older cousin's boyfriend saw me standing at the doorway of the room, unable to walk across the threshold. I knew him from Sunday dinners and Christmas Eve celebrations so when Paul came over to talk to me, I managed to eke out a small smile.

"Are you ok?" he asked. "What do you need?"

"I don't want to see him in the casket. I don't want to touch his body but I wrote this letter for him," I managed to say softly.

"I'll go in with you if you want."

"You will? Are you sure?"

He smiled and gave me a hug. "I've got you," he said as he held my hand and walked me into the room. I looked at the casket only to see my grandmother sobbing as she was bent over the casket laying her chest across his.

What the fuck is she doing was all I could think. I stopped in my tracks and stared. Paul didn't miss a beat. "It's okay. She's hurting. People grieve in different ways," he started to explain.

I saw my dad come to his mother's side and take her away from my grandfather to sit at the chair placed at the end of his casket. It was going to be a long few days so the funeral home set out a chair for her to take breaks.

Paul stood by my side as I made my way to the casket. He gave me some space as I knelt on the kneeler to talk to him one last time. I thanked my grandfather and told him I would miss him. He looked so peaceful and also like he was wearing too much makeup. But dead people, right? I held the letter in my hand, unable to bring myself to touch a dead body. His hands were crossed. Those bent fingers. Paul was at my side and asked me if I wanted him to put the letter in my grandfather's suit pocket.

Dear Grandpa Joe,

I really didn't get an opportunity to say goodbye. I saw you before your surgery and I talked to you after, but I never thought that I would never be able to hear or see you alive again. I just want to take a minute to tell you why you're one of the greatest men I've ever known.

You have always done things for me. You brightened my day with your phone calls and visits, especially when you brought homemade pasta. At your age, the things you did never ceased to amaze me.

I watered your garden today, don't worry, everything is fine. I'm going to miss your homemade pasta. I hope Gram can make it as good as you. I'm really going to miss you. I just want you to know that I love you and I'm going to miss everything you do for me.

Pray for me in heaven. I am going to need it and pray for the family. We all miss you.

Take care and I love you always and forever.

Your loving granddaughter, Chrissy

"Please and thanks Paul. Thank you."

Reading that letter now, I see it. "I watered your garden today, don't worry, everything is fine."

I was 12 and already trying to fix things. Already trying to take care of everyone else. I was reassuring people that everything was fine when nothing was fine.

That's when it started. I just didn't know it yet.

The next big death in our family was 10 years later. My aunt died in her early 50s from recurrent breast cancer. She was my mom's only sister and this was the beginning of a long journey of grief for my mom. My aunt's second battle with breast cancer only lasted 10 months and it was brutal. Our whole family was traumatized in some way as we watched cancer ravage her brain.

One of my most vivid memories was a call from my dad, asking me about the legality of advanced directives because some family members were questioning her wishes.

"Chrissy, your aunt's wishes are to provide life-saving measures. She checked the boxes for breathing tubes, supplemental nutrition, and resuscitation if her heart stops. But your grandmother is trying to argue against these things. She doesn't want her daughter to suffer."

"Who is her medical power of attorney?"

"Your mom and she's torn."

I was halfway through my second year of law school and had spent a year of graduate school in Italy studying medical ethics. This was my thing. But here I was, detached, talking about the issues in a clinical way, shoving down any connection to the fact we were talking about my aunt.

"Tell Mom she has to respect what's on that document. I know this is killing Grammy, but it's not her choice to make."

My dad knew all of this, but I think he was grasping, feeling torn for his wife and heartbroken for my aunt. None of it mattered in the end. She passed the next afternoon. Three months later, my grandfather had a heart attack at 83.

My mom's parents were married nearly 60 years. They survived being separated during WWII and once my grandfather returned home from the war, they never really spent time apart. When my grandfather collapsed at home, my grandmother managed to call 911 and the EMTs were able to get him to the hospital in time. He had a stent placed and was stable.

It was a Saturday in January and I had just driven to DC to see Mark. I had a few days left of my Christmas break before I returned to my second semester of my second year of law school. My grandfather and I loved to talk about the Steelers so I wanted to check on him and talk about the game on Sunday. It was about four in the afternoon and I called the hospital switchboard asking to be transferred to his room.

Ring. Ring. A female voice answered.

"Oh I am sorry. I must have the wrong room. I asked to be connected to my grandfather's room," I said.

"Who is your grandfather?" she asked. I told her his name.

"This is his nurse. What's your name and number? The doctors are working on him right now and I'll have someone call you back soon."

I gave her my information. The doctors are working ON him? Shit. He's dead. I turned to Mark because I was staying with him. "My grandfather is dead."

"What? I thought he was going to be okay? Is that what they said on the phone?"

"No, not exactly. The nurse said the doctors are working ON him. You don't work ON someone unless you're trying to save them." I knew this in my bones.

Thirty minutes or so passed and my phone rang. It was a 412 area code - Pittsburgh. It must be the hospital. My hands were shaking.

"Hello," I answered.

"Is this Chrissy? I'm Dr. Stratford. I am sorry to tell you but your grandfather didn't make it. Your family had just left and it looks like he had another heart attack. We tried everything we could but we weren't able to save him. I am sorry."

"Thank you for trying."

"I'm going to call his wife now."

"No please don't. I will call my dad. He's with my mom and grandmother now. I can tell him."

"Are you sure? I don't want you to have to do that."

"Yes I'm sure. It will be better coming from me. Thank you, Doctor."

He hung up and I still had the phone to my ear. I was frozen. How the hell am I going to tell my parents this?

I took a deep breath and called my dad. He answered quickly, knowing I was driving to DC, so he probably thought I was just checking in to tell them I arrived safely.

"Hi honey. How was the drive?"

"It was fine. No traffic. Where are you guys?"

"We just got seated for dinner. Spent the afternoon at the hospital and your mom and grandmother are starving. You know they wouldn't willingly eat hospital cafeteria food."

"Dad, I have something to tell you. Pop is gone," I said with a shaky voice.

"What are you talking about? We just left him. He was fine."

"The doctor just called me. It happened right after you guys left. Knowing Pop, he was probably waiting for you all to go. He died, Dad."

I heard my mom frantically asking what was going on. I could picture them sitting at this restaurant and knowing what was coming next...screams. My mom and my grandmother were screaming "NO! NO! NO!" "WE JUST SAW HIM! HE WAS FINE!" in the restaurant. I could barely hear my dad say goodbye over their screams.

I had to go back to Pittsburgh and so I kissed Mark goodbye and got in my car for another four-hour drive.

Losing my aunt and my grandfather within the span of three months was hard. For my mom to bury her sister and her dad, it was too much. This was the beginning of her grief journey and spiral into depression, which would change her from the mom I knew to one I didn't recognize at the end.

Nine years later, in 2011, my family would break.

Cancer is brutal. There's no question this insidious disease destroys lives, terrorizes families and leaves massive trauma in its wake. My dad's aunt, my great aunt, was battling pancreatic cancer. Aunt Rose was like a third grandmother to me. She was the youngest girl in her family of five and for as tough and mean as my grandmother was, my aunt was gentle and kind. She was nearing the end of her battle and my dad was beginning his.

It was an average April Wednesday morning when my life changed forever. I was getting ready for work, going about my normal morning routine when my phone rang - a 412 area code again. Is this deja vu?

"Hello."

"Is this Chrissy?"

"Yes, this is she."

"Chrissy, this is Dr. Mitchell. I'm your dad's primary care physician. As you know he came to the hospital last night and we kept him to run some tests. Those tests are back." He paused and then continued.

"I am afraid it's not good news," he said with a gentle calmness as he was about to deliver news that would shatter my family.

"Your dad has cancer. We did a CT scan and it lit up like a Christmas tree. It looks like it is in his spine, lungs, liver, and kidneys. You need to come home. And your dad wanted me to tell you to please ignore your mother's calls, or if you do talk to her, do not tell her anything. She is driving to the hospital now and he doesn't want her to worry while she's driving," he pleaded.

For the life of me I can't remember if I spoke to my dad or what I said in response other than I would leave soon and it would take me four hours to drive from DC.

I had been working in healthcare for six years, and just a few months prior, I began working at a cancer center. Like so many, cancer had touched our family, and I wanted to work in an area that was meaningful and personal. Little did I know this career choice would shape so much of my life, both good and bad.

I immediately called my boss to give him the news about my father. "Go home and be with your family. That is the most important thing right now. Do not worry about work. Just keep me posted and I am here if you need anything," he said.

Thank you didn't seem like enough of a response, but as I thanked him and hung up the phone, it immediately began to ring again as my mom's number flashed on the screen. Ignore.

I called my brother and told him everything the doctor said. I let him know that I would be driving home and would meet him at the hospital in a few hours. I spoke with no emotion. No tears. Only a flat voice arranging the next few hours as if they were any other morning. I didn't stay on the phone long enough to have a meaningful conversation, just reminding him that whatever he did next, he wasn't to tell my mom anything.

My phone buzzed again and it was my mom. Shit. I had to answer it. "Hi Mom. Are you heading into the hospital?"

"Yes I'm driving now. Have you talked to Dad? I keep trying his cell phone and he's not picking up," she said, sounding worried. She should be.

"No Mom. I haven't talked to him yet today. I'm sure they're just busy with tests and he can't talk right now. I wouldn't worry," I tried to assure her.

Damn this sucked. I felt horrible lying but I knew my dad was right about not telling her the truth right now. My mom wasn't one to handle bad news well. Since she had lost her sister and her dad a number of years ago, she hadn't been the same. The signs were small at first, then impossible to ignore. She snapped more easily, mostly at me. She fought going to social events, unless it was Friday night movies with my dad. She let herself fade, but through it all, she stayed close to my father as if he were the last solid thing left.

She didn't seem to be calmed by my plea to not worry. She needed gentleness. I left her with instructions as I had to pack and get on the road.

"Mom, give me a call when you get to the hospital and know more. I have to get to work, but I'll keep my cell phone on." Of course I couldn't tell her I was on my way to Pittsburgh. Another lie.

I packed a bag and got Scooby ready to go. I rescued Scooby from Ryan's family as his uncle's kids had grown tired of the dog and wanted a new puppy. The family planned to take him to a shelter, and after meeting him that Thanksgiving weekend, I knew there was no way I was letting that happen. He was around nine years old when I gave him a new home, and he warmed his way into the spot of my best friend. My dad had a fondness for him too, as he had always wanted a dog when he was little but my grandmother wasn't having it. I wasn't sure how long I'd be home, so I packed enough for the weekend. I could always do laundry at my parents' house.

Everything was packed and ready to go, but I decided to run to the bathroom once more before heading out. Rush hour traffic getting out of DC was a nightmare, and with a few cups of coffee in me, I didn't want to have to get off the highway for a pit stop. Just as I was pulling up my pants I heard a sound, and immediately realized I had put my phone in the back pocket of my jeans, and now, my phone was in the toilet. "You've got to be fucking kidding me," I yelled.

I fished it out, trying the hair dryer trick. The screen was black. I needed to be on the road and I needed a working phone. I grabbed Scooby and walked to the Verizon store a few blocks away.

As the store opened, I word-vomited all over the sales clerk. "My dad has cancer…I dropped my phone in the toilet… I need to drive four hours home. Can you please fix this fast?"

For the first time my eyes started to mist while I waited. The clerk looked it over and told me my phone couldn't be saved. There was too much water damage. The manager overheard our conversation and walked over. "My mom had cancer," he said. "I'm going to give you a new phone, no charge."

"I can pay. You don't need to do that."

He wouldn't hear of it.

I saw the pity in his eyes, and I thanked him again, wanting to get out of there as fast as possible. I needed to get on the road.

As I reached the door, he called after me. "I'll keep your father in my prayers."

I nodded and left. Prayers weren't going to save my father. I knew it in the deepest part of myself.

A few weeks later I was standing in the funeral home for my Aunt Rose's viewing. My parents didn't go as my dad was too sick and my mom couldn't handle facing people's questions about how he was doing. I was asked to read something before they closed the casket and we all headed to the Church for the funeral mass.

Like I had done countless times in my life, I stood in front of the room and spoke, loud, clear, and even paced. I don't get nervous speaking in front of people, never have, so I didn't see this as different than any other time I'd given a presentation, read at Mass or even when I was on TV for my old job.

One of my aunts came up to me after I was finished and gave me a hug. She said I did a beautiful job and then she asked, "Do you eat nails for breakfast?"

WHAT THE FUCK DID SHE JUST SAY? I know I haven't slept well lately, but there was no way she just said that. I didn't respond, just staring at her blankly.

"Do you eat nails for breakfast?" she asked again when I just stared at her in silence.

Those words hardened something in me. She meant it as a compliment and I took it as one. I didn't cry. I wasn't falling apart even though my world as I knew it was crumbling around me. I was single and in my early 30s. I could do this and I didn't need anyone.

I became the strong one who doesn't break. I got shit done and handled everything. And people kept praising me for it. Death after death. All I heard was "You're so strong." "I don't know how you do it." "You're amazing." I wore this praise like armor. I believed it protected me.

But I realize now that being praised for not grieving taught me that grieving was weakness. Crying was a failure. Remember, I am Generation X. The generation that was raised in a culture to prioritize toughness. We weren't taught how to be in touch with our feelings.

So I just... didn't. I didn't cry. I didn't need to be coddled because I would never break. But I'm not strong. I'm just performing.

Performing strength so no one sees how much I'm carrying. Because if they saw through me, they'd know that I'm not made of nails. I'm just broken. And I feel like I'm holding it together through sheer force of will.

A few weeks later, when the doctor finally told my dad that he should consider hospice, he did so with the explanation that anyone can come off of hospice and that this decision wasn't permanent. It would allow him to have more supportive care services and keep him comfortable. My dad still wasn't ready to die and this was the only way to get him to agree. I knew he wasn't going to make it. He was still in denial. Reluctantly my dad agreed to this next step with my encouragement.

The hospital helped to identify a facility just 15 minutes from my parents' home, making it more convenient to spend time with him. The ambulance would transfer him and my mom and I would meet him there.

We said our goodbyes to his care team and thanked them for helping my dad through this journey. Working in cancer, I knew he wouldn't be seeing his doctor again as death was coming soon. I didn't share that with my mom because I think she was holding on to the same hope as my dad, that he could be in hospice for a bit to gain some strength and then keep getting treatment.

We told my dad that we were going to head home to get some comfortable sweats and shirts for him, as he had been in a hospital gown for the last few weeks, and that we would see him in a few hours.

I don't remember much about the drive home. Did Mom and I talk? Did she just cry? For the life of me I can't recall what happened from when we left the hospital. I do remember my mom was taking her sweet ass time to gather my dad some clothes, and while we were still at their house, my cell phone rang with a local number that I didn't recognize. At this point, I was answering any call that came my way as no doubt in some way it was about my dad's health, his office, his insurance…. It was actually my dad on the line, angry and impatient.

"Where the hell are you guys? You said you'd be here." I could hear the fear in his voice. We promised him he wouldn't be alone and we were already breaking that promise. I told him we were leaving the house any minute and would be there in 15 minutes.

"Hurry up." And then he hung up.

Rushing my mom, I told her we had to go. I think she was being deliberately slow because seeing Dad in the hospice facility would make this hellish reality real.

We pulled up to the facility and parked close to the front entrance. It was a warm July day and we got there late in the afternoon. I held out my arm for my mom to hold onto as the last thing I needed was for her to go down. She had been known to trip and fall here and there.

Walking up to the front desk, I asked for my dad's room. The receptionist had a warmth in her eyes as she looked at her computer. She found his name and said she would take us there. As she walked from around the desk and came to lead us to his room, I noticed she couldn't be much older than my dad in his mid-60s. I wondered what would make someone want a job like this. Having to greet people who were undoubtedly in the throes of hell visiting a loved one on deathwatch.

She walked us to my dad's room and I thanked her for her kindness and then she touched my arm before walking away. A gentle gesture that brought me comfort. People who work in hospice are cut from a different cloth. They are the best of society in every way.

My mom didn't say anything, She just fiddled with the bag of clothes she had in her hand. I took a deep breath before walking into my dad's room and putting on a smile. The room was larger than I had anticipated. It was a deep maroon color with dark wood trim. To the right of the door was my dad's bed and on the other side of the room were two chairs for visitors. The room also had a TV mounted to the wall above a shelf with a sink and the bathroom tucked in the corner. This place, while filled with sickness and death, felt comforting and not nearly as clinical as the hospital had been for the last three weeks. I tried to sound cheery when I greeted my dad but it didn't appear he was in the mood for small talk. He was a shell of himself physically, and the man with the personality as big as the moon was quiet and reserved. My mom immediately began fussing over him, showing him all of the clothes she brought him.

I don't remember how long we were in the room before a nurse walked in and introduced herself. I don't remember her name but she addressed my dad first and then us. He was her priority and that was refreshing to see. Once she was assured my dad was comfortable and didn't need anything at the moment, she turned to me and Mom and said she had some paperwork for us to fill out. She asked which one of us was the healthcare proxy and I answered that we both were. She handed the paperwork to my mom and said they needed to be filled out before we left.

My mom stared at the clipboard and didn't move for a moment.

"I can't sign these. You do it." Mom handed me the clipboard. There were no tears, just denial and fear. She walked over to my dad and sat on the bed with him.

I was left standing alone, holding the paperwork, knowing this was one more thing I had to do because my mom couldn't.

I read through everything and realized part of what I was signing was standard hospice paperwork for Medicare and the other pages were advance directives. I was about to sign the Do No Resuscitate order for my dad, which meant if he stopped breathing for any reason, they would let him die. No CPR. Nothing. His cancer was going to take his life no matter what, but when? How much more time would we have if he did need CPR? I was going to be the one that made this decision because my mom couldn't do it.

If I didn't sign the DNR and they had to perform CPR, what state would he be in? He was so frail already and what kind of damage would that do to his body? If he needed CPR and I had signed the DNR he would be gone. I was damned either way and so was he.

After we received my dad's diagnosis, I remember calling my parents from my apartment in DC. I was sitting at the kitchen table as I knew the best chance I had with this conversation was to not be in front of them when I brought it up; however, that was wishful thinking. I told my dad he needed to create his healthcare wishes. Did he want to be resuscitated? Did he want a feeding tube? Did he want to be put on a ventilator?

How could he forget what happened with my aunt?

Because of my background in healthcare and law, I understood the importance of these conversations. They help clinicians, they protect families, and they prevent moments like the one I was living. Forced to decide for him simply because he couldn't bring himself to talk about it, as if avoiding the topic could keep his cancer from becoming real.

My dad was calling to me from the other side of the room asking me what I was doing. He asked what the paperwork said. There was no way in hell I was going to tell him what I was doing. If he couldn't handle the conversation when he was healthier, there was no way I was going to take what little hope he clung to away, as much as I would have given anything to have him make this choice, and not me.

"Nothing, Dad. It's just standard intake forms. I'll fill them out and give them back to the nurse," I said without any emotion.

That was the only way I was going to survive this. Put up the walls and just get shit done. It's what I always did and this time would be no different. I signed the paperwork and found the nurse in the hallway. It's like the longer I held them in my hands, the more I felt the weight of my actions. I don't remember anything else from that day.

Five days later he was gone. I planned my dad's funeral. Picked out his urn. His clothes. Chose the readings for his funeral mass. I was the one comforting my mom. My brother had a wife so I didn't worry about him. I didn't worry about myself. I worked in cancer and I knew this day was coming. And when it did, I barely cried.

Over the next 14 years, I lost my two grandmothers, my dog Scooby, one of my childhood best friends, my uncle, three friends, and my mom. So much death and I got through it the same way I had learned. To move forward and move on. I may have cried a little here and there, but the paralyzing grief, the one where people can't seem to get out of bed, or to eat, or the one where they cry all the time… I don't understand that. I don't do weakness. I eat nails for breakfast, remember?

My mom spent 12 years after my dad died living in paralyzing grief. She didn't know how to move forward and lived with severe depression. She made a few attempts to rebuild but nothing lasted and she didn't try to find joy or meaning beyond the loss. She just existed in her grief. It was the only thing left of her. Not even her young grandchildren could bring a lasting spark.

I hated watching it. I loathed that she let grief destroy her. I saw it as a weakness not to seek help or grief support. I tried relentlessly to get her to talk to someone. I was fucking pissed that she gave up.

After my dad died, when I started facing my own losses, I vowed I would never grieve like her. It would not paralyze me. Giving up is never an option. I would be STRONG. I would eat nails for breakfast and push though. And that's exactly what I did for years. Loss after loss. I just kept going.

I carried the belief that made me stronger than her. Better than her because I wouldn't let it paralyze me. But I'm starting to realize that I'm not better. I'm just scared. Scared of letting grief win and looking weak. So I made sure I never grieved at all.

It wasn't just grief I learned to handle alone. I was learning that one of the foundational tethers in my life would eventually let me down.

Part Three:

Breaking and Rebuilding

Chapter 7: *Losing Your Anchor*

I was raised Catholic, which meant attending Mass on Sundays and holy days of obligation. I also went to Catholic grade school, high school, and then college and graduate school in Rome. I was connected to my faith, though I wouldn't describe myself as devout. I found comfort in the soothing rituals. The smell of incense at Mass, the rhythm of prayer, and the familiar hymns all made me feel grounded and connected. *Be Not Afraid* was one of my favorites.

Being Catholic meant belonging to a community. I'd see my classmates at school and again at Mass on Sundays. We attended church festivals and participated in volunteer opportunities. It was a built-in social network.

I came from an Irish-Italian family, which is like being double Catholic. My Italian grandmother wore an obscenely large medallion of Padre Pio, a saint from Italy, and my Irish grandfather carried the same rosary with him from WWII until he died.

I spent decades as a Catholic without ever actively choosing it. It was simply what I did because it was expected and it was familiar. I was born into it, and that shaped everything about how I practiced or didn't practice my faith.

As a young adult, I started questioning everything. When I chose to attend a Catholic college, it was more because I couldn't wait to experience Washington, DC, and less about the school being Catholic. It was four hours from Pittsburgh, close enough to come home and far enough away to gain the independence I so desperately craved.

On my first day of college orientation a few blocks from school, my family was in a serious car accident, landing my mom in the hospital with almost 80 stitches in her head. My brother and my dad had minor injuries and I luckily came through unscathed. When I finally got to campus, shaken and exhausted, my room was already set up. My boxes were unpacked. My sheets were washed and on the bed. My computer sat on my desk, unharmed. The campus priest, Father John, had organized it all. That kind of compassion was what Catholicism meant to me.

After this, Father John made it a point to look out for me. When his friend Mother Teresa was visiting the US, making a stop in DC, he included me with a small group of students to attend Mass and meet her. I remember walking into a large, bare room filled with folding chairs. Nuns in white saris with blue stripes quietly took their seats. I scanned the front of the room, expecting to see her near the altar.

She wasn't there. She was in the back corner, kneeling, praying the entire time. It was almost as if she was hidden, trying to be invisible from onlookers.

After Mass, she stood at the door and greeted each person. When it was my turn, she took my hands, prayed over me, and placed a Miraculous Medal in my palm. At the time, I didn't understand the weight of that moment. I was being blessed by a future saint. Years later, after my dad was diagnosed with cancer, I found the medal with my rosary. My father had strong faith and asked if he could have it, as he needed a miracle. Of course I said yes. I didn't believe it would do anything, but if it comforted him, that was enough.

I was a philosophy major in college and I suppose my discernment began then. This major, which ensures unemployment unless you go to grad school, trains you to value questions more than answers. You learn to question authority thoughtfully. At its deepest levels, philosophy is inward-looking. It guides you to know yourself through reflection.

While I attended Mass weekly, sometimes even daily, I was starting to doubt what I'd been taught. And it started with a new friend I made in my dorm.

Oliver quickly became a close friend during the first few months of our freshman year. We often spent time on the weekends exploring the city, hopping on the subway, picking a stop and roaming the streets.

After a few weeks I could tell he was clearly wrestling with something.

"Is something bothering you? You seem off today," I asked, sensing he wanted to talk.

"Yeah, I was just thinking about something. How do you feel about gays?"

I didn't hesitate. "That's gross. It's wrong. Catholics don't accept that." I was just saying what I learned from others and from the Church.

He went quiet and immediately changed the subject. We didn't talk about it again for months. And I didn't think anything of it. I didn't know anyone who was out so I didn't know what I didn't know.

A few months passed and our friendship continued to grow. We were on another weekend adventure in the city along the National Mall. We stopped for a little picnic.

"I need to tell you something. I'm not sure how you're going to react."

I could tell he was nervous. "Uh. Okay. You're scaring me."

"Well, I'm a little scared about how you're going to react."

"What is it? You can tell me anything."

"I'm gay."

"You're gay?" I said it like a question, like I was processing.

"Yeah. I'm gay."

I sat there for a second, thinking about what I'd said months ago. Fuck. I can't believe I said that.

"Ok, cool. I'm... I'm sorry for what I said before. That was really shitty."

"You're okay with this? A few months ago you told me it was gross. I've been terrified to tell you for months. But the closer friends we became, I couldn't keep lying to you anymore."

"I am sorry. I was ignorant before. You're the first gay person I've ever known. I am so sorry I hurt you."

I understood why he'd gone silent all those months. I'd hurt him, and he'd been carrying that. I felt like shit. Not because the Church told me to accept gays as long as they don't act on it, but because I'd hurt someone I cared about by spouting off beliefs I'd never actually questioned. This was the mid-90s. Homosexuality was becoming more visible, but it wasn't widely accepted. I was raised to think it was wrong, and I never questioned it.

He understood. He'd been raised an Irish Catholic. He forgave me but I never forgot that moment. It was the first time I realized that everything I'd learned in church might not be true. Once I started questioning one thing, it was hard to stop.

Take sex, for example. My mom never had the sex talk, and I went to Catholic school, so I definitely didn't hear about it there. The only messages I ever got were "If you get pregnant, we will kill you" and "premarital sex is a sin." But I was in college.

Everyone around me was sleeping around. Was it really as bad as I'd been taught?

Questioning the Church's teachings should have felt monumental. I could have prayed about it, talked to a priest, or turned to the teachings of the Church. That's what you're supposed to do when your faith is tested. But I didn't. I didn't pray or talk about it with anyone. Hell, I didn't even own a Bible. I just kept questioning. And it was that easy, which probably should have been a sign of what was to come.

Law school only bolstered my resolve in questioning my faith. It trains you to strip emotion out of a situation and focus on facts, rules and outcomes. As students you learn how to argue both sides and to always assume there's a counterargument. There is rarely a right answer, so you learn to live in the gray areas.

As a Catholic, you aren't taught to question. You're taught to blindly believe. Believe that a priest in a confessional booth has the power to forgive your sins through absolution and penance. Believe that only men are given the divine right to be leaders in the Church. Believe that priests, who are forbidden from getting married, could one day counsel you through marriage troubles. Believe that gays are children of God but that acting on their sexuality is a sin. Believe that life begins with conception and that abortion is the killing of a defenseless life and is a sin.

You are also taught to believe priests are trustworthy. Which is laughable now that we know about decades of massive sexual abuse.

In the early 2000s, the Boston Globe exposed widespread sexual abuse and coverup by priests and Church leaders. This happened while I was in law school. I immediately left the Church when these stories came to light. I never questioned whether this was the right decision because I knew for me, it just was.

In 2018, the state of Pennsylvania released the names of the accused priests. I was curious to see if I knew anyone. I was hoping I wouldn't find a recognizable name, but somewhere deep down, I think somehow I knew I would.

Fuck. My old parish priest was on the list. He heard my confessions when I was a kid. I then thought about the times other kids were alone with him. What he was accused of doing to them. I wanted to throw up. I was so disgusted and angry. Did I know anyone he abused? My brother was an altar boy when he was little. Did something happen to him?

I immediately picked up the phone to call my brother. My nerves had me rattled.

He answered on the second ring.

"Did you see the news?" I asked. "The Pennsylvania list of priests?"

"Yeah." His voice was flat.

I took a breath. "Father Thompson is on it. Our old parish priest."

Silence.

"I know this is a weird question, but... did he ever..." I couldn't finish the sentence.

"No," my brother said quickly. "Nothing happened to me."

Relief flooded through me. "Okay. Good. I just… I had to ask."

"I know. I'm glad you did."

But this priest wasn't the only one. There was another name too. A bishop who had been at my high school. I attended his Masses. And a cardinal I'd met during college. All disgraced. All accused or complicit. These weren't priests in some distant city. These were men from my childhood. They were men I knew personally, not just a name on paper.

The ease and swiftness with which I left should have told me something. People with real faith struggled with this scandal. They wrestled with their faith and found ways to stay despite the horror of what the Church had done. But me? I was relieved. This gave me a legitimate reason to leave. I didn't have to explain myself. There was no need to defend my faith. I could just say 'I can't support an institution that did this' and no one could argue.

Looking back, I spent my entire childhood and my early 20s as a Catholic. Law school was the first time I had been in a secular educational setting. My life was surrounded by Catholicism. And what did I get from all of those years?

I didn't have a strong faith in Catholic teachings. I didn't have a spiritual anchor in my life, praying only when I needed something. My faith didn't give me a sense of purpose or meaning. Not because the Church couldn't give those things, but because I never let it. I went to Mass. I participated but didn't really connect.

When I left, I didn't replace it with anything. I just stopped practicing religion. After walking away from the only spiritual community I'd ever known, I decided that I was fine. There is no need for something like that in my life.

But maybe I was just proving what I'd always believed, that I was better off alone. Investing in something always means risking disappointment. I relied on my security blanket of going through the motions rather than to actually care.

When I walked away from the Church, I didn't miss it. I didn't grieve the loss of my relationship with God, likely because it was never that strong to begin with. I just moved on and never looked back.

Which probably says everything.

I never found another anchor. I didn't seek out another religious denomination. I didn't find meaning or purpose in anything spiritual. I just left and with it a void filled the space. I'm not sure if that's because I didn't think I could find something that was a better fit or because I never really tried. I missed the sense of community over the years, but not enough to forgive the Church for betraying my trust.

The Church wasn't the only place I couldn't find where I belonged. I was walking away from friendships too. And I couldn't figure out how to stop.

Chapter 8: *When You Fight for It*

Sarah and I met in my senior year of college, when I was an RA. I loved that job. Some women on my floor kept to themselves, some came to me for advice, some just wanted a friendly face. And one, unexpectedly, became my sister.

Sarah was a sophomore who lived at the end of the hall with three of her friends. She was loud, funny, and a free spirit in a way I was not. She danced down the hallway and blasted music even during quiet hours. At first she drove me insane. I didn't want to be the enforcer. I wanted trust more than rules. I'd supported residents through rape, suicidal thoughts, traumatic childhoods, identity crises, expulsions, and endless noise complaints. Yet somehow, the one who changed me most was the girl blasting music and dancing in the hallway.

She cracked something open in me. I'd spent years living up to this expectation set by my parents, always concerned about how people viewed me. She taught me about joy and living in the moment. She taught me that sometimes rules are meant to be broken. I don't remember the first real conversation we had. I just remember that at some point, she was suddenly everywhere in my life.

That winter, we went out for her birthday. I was 21 and she wasn't. I never liked being around my underage residents while they were drinking. Again, rule follower. But I made an exception that night. There was bar hopping, dancing, and way too much alcohol. It was the kind of night where someone in the group was going to end up hugging the toilet. As the cab dropped us back at our dorm, I remember half walking, half dragging her up the stairs, making sure she had enough water and Tylenol before she passed out. Later, back in my room, I remember sitting on my bed and realizing how I'd never really had a night like that. I'd never let myself just be, without worrying what anyone thought. She made it feel safe to explore this untapped side of me.

After I graduated, distance didn't matter. Italy. DC. Pittsburgh. We stayed close. We emailed, called, and eventually texted once we both got cell phones. One summer during law school, we lived together, and that's when something shifted, not between us, exactly, but inside me. She started dating Scott, who lived in Chicago. I too was in a long-distance relationship but mine already began to feel like it was crumbling. I watched her fall in love while the ground was shifting under me.

I didn't handle it well. I believed that this was normal and relationships evolve. But something small and ugly was festering.

I began to compare our relationships. I measured mine against hers. I started to feel left behind even though no one had left me.

When she moved to Chicago for grad school and to be with him, I visited. It was a bonus that she and Patrick, one of my childhood best friends, lived in the same city. I got a twofer when I spent time there. We did all the fun things you do in your 20s. Cubs games in the summer, rooftop happy hours, and an obscene amount of layers in the winter to head out to the bars. We had so much fun, but through it all, I kept tallying my life against hers.

The night she called to tell me Scott had proposed, I was home visiting my parents, lying on their couch watching some Hallmark movie. I said all the right things. I was happy for her. But after we hung up, I cried.

Everyone in my life was moving forward and I felt like I was standing still. When she asked me to be her maid of honor, I said yes immediately. This felt more special than the other times I'd been a maid of honor. This was Sarah. But I couldn't shake the feeling that I was about to lose my best friend to a guy, for the second time.

I had trouble keeping a guy around for longer than a few months, let alone someone worthy of marriage. And here I was, standing up for her perfect love story while mine was falling apart. How was I going to put my own selfish feelings aside? How awful of me to make this about me.

I did my best to put my own insecurities to the side, but I am guessing I did a shitty job. After she got married, and then pregnant, our lives began to look nothing alike. She was building a family and I was surrounding myself with men who could not love me. By then, I was with Ryan. Things were bad. It was worse than I was willing to admit to anyone and I didn't want her to see any of it. I couldn't stomach having to explain how far I had drifted from the girl she knew.

So I did what I had been doing all of my life, and I disappeared. I accepted that this was a normal part of friendships, that they change when someone starts a family. Married people gravitate toward other married people and when you have kids, forget it. All you want to do is talk about your child. In truth though, the distance was because of shame. I didn't call. I let years pass.

But then, my dad got sick.

Sarah had known my family over the years, staying at my parents' house to break up the drive from Chicago to DC. My dad played the trumpet at her wedding. They knew her and loved her. And I missed her. This wasn't a loss that I could endure without her. But I couldn't call because if she didn't answer, I don't think I would have had the composure to leave a groveling voicemail.

I sat at my computer for an hour before I could start typing. What was I going to say? How do you apologize for years of distance? For choosing an abusive asshole over your best friend?

But my dad was dying. And I needed her. I couldn't do this alone anymore.

I started typing.

Dear Sarah,

I know this letter is long overdue. First, I want to say that I am sorry that over the past few years I let you down as a friend. I have taken a lot of time to think about how I chose to live my life and who I chose to keep in it and who I shut out and why. I feel like I owe you an explanation as well as an apology.

When I started dating Ryan, my distance really kicked in. I knew very early on, first date actually, that he was no good for me. But I was filling a void of being single for so long and watching all of my friends marry. And I was filling a void I felt in our friendship. When you and Scott moved back and bought the house, I felt relegated to an hour here and there for manicures or lunches but no real meaningful time together. I felt like you made time for his friends, hung out with married couples. I was left on the outside.

Ryan and I broke up after nearly three years together. He borrowed $4K and hasn't paid it back, he borrowed my car and damaged it, he cheated on me, he choked me one night, and held me off the ground by my neck until a neighbor heard. He made me feel scared more times than I can count.

Why did I stay? I don't know. Part of me was scared to admit I was wrong, part of me was embarrassed beyond belief. I thought I could fix him.

During the times I saw you when we were together, I couldn't bring myself to say I was anything other than super happy. I didn't know how to walk away.

I didn't fight to save our friendship because I didn't have the energy. I had given it all away over the last few years.

I am not asking for anything at this moment but forgiveness for walking out on you as a friend. I don't expect that to happen overnight. If it's not in the cards, I understand. But I wanted you to know that I was sorry for not fighting to save our friendship over the years.

I hope you and your family are well.

-Chrissy

I read it over three times. My finger hovered over the send button. This could go either way. She could read this and never respond. She could tell me it was too late. She could say she'd moved on.

I hit send. And waited.

Sarah wrote back within a few hours. Apology accepted. I told her about my dad. About the cancer and that the end was near. But I didn't ask for her to be there. I felt like it was too soon.

A few weeks later, on the morning of my father's funeral, I was standing by his casket when I saw her walk in. She was pregnant again and made what I am sure was a very uncomfortable four-hour drive from DC. My dad loved her and she was there for him, for me.

She had forgiven me. I don't remember what we said to each other that morning. I just remember her arms around me. It felt so easy again with her, even after everything.

For a long time, I told myself that it took my dad dying to bring her back into my life. But the sad truth is that I had already lost her before that, and I had done it myself. Walking away had been my armor when things felt messy or when I wasn't sure how to process my emotions. I left before anyone else could.

My dad's death didn't teach me who mattered. It showed me what it costs when you run out of time.

Sarah and I found each other again and our relationship is stronger than ever. She and Scott are my daughter's godparents. Our kids are close. We are family. I don't believe anymore that distance or pain is what separates people. I think most of the time, it's shame. There's a story we tell ourselves that the people who once knew us wouldn't understand who we've become.

But I think my most important lesson of all is that I shouldn't have walked away in the first place. I shouldn't have waited until my dad was dying to own my part in letting our friendship end. For fuck's sake, it shouldn't have taken death to give me clarity about life, but sometimes that's how it goes during a crisis.

Living the lesson when there's no crisis? That's the hard part. Being vulnerable with others is a choice. Choosing vulnerability over protection, every single day, without the motivation of disaster? I haven't figured that one out yet.

I learned that lesson with Sarah. I fought for her and she came back. I thought that meant second chances were always possible. You could walk away and come back later, and the people who mattered would still be there.

I was wrong.

Chapter 9: *When You Don't*

Covid had everyone on pins and needles. The news was running a death tally in the corner of the screen. People were afraid to leave their homes. The world was in chaos.

And then I got an email from my aunt Judy asking if I had heard the news that my friend Patrick died.

Patrick DIED? WHAT THE FUCK?

I remember staring at the screen, knowing my eyes weren't reading this right. If she hadn't attached the obituary, I would have chalked it up to the Covid crazies everyone seemed to be suffering from.

Patrick was 45 years old and died after a valiant battle with cancer.

Cancer? Since when did Patrick have cancer?

I watched the video montage the funeral home posted. I couldn't stop crying. My chest tightened and my heart started racing. I called my mom and told her the news. I don't know what I expected her to say. Maybe this once she would have come through for me to say something that made sense of it all. She didn't. In her defense, there was nothing she could have said. After we hung up, I slid down the wall and started hyperventilating. My chest tightened. I felt like I was having a heart attack.

My daughter Mia heard me crying, gasping for air. She was almost three and didn't understand what was happening. She ran to get Irwin. I told him through sobs that one of my childhood best friends died and that my chest hurt and I thought something was really wrong.

We decided I should go to urgent care but I had to go alone. There was no way I was bringing a toddler into a medical building during Covid. She was too little and we were being extra cautious.

When you walk into urgent care and say "chest pains," they don't make you wait. I was ushered back to an exam room and immediately hooked up to monitors. They checked my blood pressure and oxygen levels. The nurse left the room and I sat there waiting. I already had a bit of healthcare anxiety, so sitting here alone, with this heavy grief and now the potential of having a heart attack, was too much. I started breathing heavily again.

After what felt like an eternity, a doctor walked in to give me my results. "Everything is normal," he said. No signs of a heart attack. But I didn't feel normal. I felt like I was dying.

The nurse came back into the room and asked me what I had been doing when it started. I told her about my aunt's email. I told her about Mia at home. And then she did something extraordinary. She pulled up a chair and asked me to tell her about Patrick. We were both masked so all I could see were her eyes. They were so kind and caring. She took my hand and let me cry. She said it sounded like I had a panic attack, which made sense given the news about Patrick. Her eyes were glassy. I couldn't tell if she was tired or sad for me. Or maybe she was just carrying too much because of Covid. But the way she sat there with me, it calmed me.

When I got home, I told Irwin it was likely a panic attack. And then I didn't cry after that.

That's pretty much how my grief works. I have a quick cry and then I'm done. My eyes might mist when a memory hits out of nowhere, or when something reminds me of the person I've lost. But I don't stay in those tears. I never saw the point. They're gone. They aren't coming back, and my tears don't change that.

What I couldn't shake was the guilt. Patrick was dead and I hadn't called. One of these days became never, and now there was nothing left to do with that except carry it.

The next day I got a Facebook message from Patrick's wife. I was married now and the name on my account changed, so she was asking if I was the same person who was the best man for her wedding. She told me Patrick had died from cancer. She said they built a beautiful life together and she held him as he passed. I was gutted. But her message also brought me so much comfort. He died a happy man with a beautiful family by his side.

Patrick and I met when I was 13. He was my cousin Rob's neighbor and friend. I would see him whenever we went to my aunt and uncle's house. This was the late 80s and early 90s so I usually found Patrick and Rob either outside playing in the cul de sac or playing Nintendo. Patrick and I both played tennis so that immediately became something we bonded over.

He was two years older than me and we went to different schools. So that meant when he got his license, it became easier to spend time together. He became my freedom. In the summers, we played a lot of tennis. We went to the mall. But our favorite hangout was Kings Diner, a hometown spot where we would spend hours talking and arguing about everything.

My parents loved Patrick so when he would show up at their house on a Saturday night at 10 o'clock asking if I wanted to go to Kings, they never hesitated to say yes. We had our favorite booth and would settle in for hours. Coffee after coffee. Sometimes we would be there so long, we'd end up ordering food. Since the diner was open 24/7, we were never in a rush to leave. Sometimes it would be one or two in the morning when he'd drop me back home.

Patrick and I talked about everything and anything. He was the person I shared everything with. He knew about Lauren. I shared my insecurities about my weight and my looks with him. He knew when I had a crush on a boy or when my parents were driving me insane. And never once did he make me feel less than or that my feelings were invalid. He had an air of ease in which he was able to let that kind of stuff roll right off, and I was jealous of that.

I remember one night, we were at the diner and I was going on about my latest crush. I was a sophomore, him a senior. After listening to me gush over a boy, he looked at me with a serious look in his eyes and said, "Guys and girls can never really be just friends."

"Um that's exactly what we are," I argued.

He continued to say that it's not possible because at some point during their friendship, one person would develop feelings. I vehemently disagreed. I got along well with guys and had friends that I was never attracted to. But his point was that maybe they were attracted to me and I just never knew.

Patrick and my relationship never crossed the boundaries of friendship. We were the exception to his rule.

Our diner debates covered every topic you can imagine. I remember when I was home visiting from college and we met up for one of our late-night antics, I told him I was going to school in Italy for grad school and we proceeded to argue for hours over the value of travelling abroad. I wanted to see the world. He said I should explore the US first. We debated like it mattered, like we were unknowingly preparing for our future. I guess it made sense we both ended up becoming lawyers.

In high school and college, Patrick worked at the local grocery store's photo department and I found myself jumping at the chance to go with either my mom or dad when they were running errands just on the off chance he was working. I'd talk to him while they shopped. There was one time his job saved my ass.

I studied Italian in high school and I had to prepare a presentation on my family's ties to Italy. My grandfather had passed away and I remember interviewing my grandmother to prepare. She gave me five photo albums filled with pictures, most notably of the last time they visited their hometown. She said I could take them to school for my presentation. After my presentation, I left them in my locker at school. They sat there for months until I had to clean it out when school ended.

I remember throwing everything from my locker into a garbage bag at the end of the year and just dumping it in my parents' garage. My locker was full of books, clothes, papers, and those photo albums, so the bag looked pretty full. I didn't think anything of leaving it in the garage, because I was a careless teenager and didn't pay much attention to the messes I left in my wake. My dad threw the bag out, thinking it was trash.

A few weeks into summer my grandmother asked for the photo albums. She had cousins coming to visit from out of town and wanted to share memories of my grandfather. I went to the garage looking for that bag from my locker but it was gone. I asked my parents if they had seen it and my dad vaguely remembered throwing out the bag. I was fucked. How was I going to explain this to my grandmother? My grandfather had been gone for a few years, and she was still dressing only in black, still in mourning.

I told Patrick what happened, not thinking he could help me, but rather just to share how stupid I was.

"What a dumbass move," he laughed to keep me from losing it and that made me laugh.

And then he continued. "Does your grandmother have the negatives for those photos?"

"I have no idea. I don't remember if they were in the albums or not."

"If you can find them, I'll just reprint the photos for you. It's easy to do."

"Holy shit you would be saving my ass. I'll look on Sunday when we go over for dinner."

Now I just had to sneak around my grandmother's house to search for the negatives. After Sunday dinner, I waited until everyone was preoccupied, clearing the table, helping with dishes, making coffee for dessert, and I went snooping.

Bingo! I found them in a drawer in her dining room. Holding the negatives up to the light, it looked like the pictures I had lost. I wasn't sure if I got all of them, but what I found would be enough to convince my grandmother, at least I hoped so.

I brought the negatives to Patrick and little by little he reprinted all of the pictures for me. I bought new photo albums and brought them over to my grandmother's. I told her the new albums were a thank you for allowing me to use them for my schoolwork. She made several comments about things seeming out of order, but other than that, no one spoke a word of it again. Patrick saved me from the wrath of my grandmother and for that, I was forever grateful.

Patrick stayed local for college but I didn't. So whenever I came home, we'd pick right back up. Always back at the same diner. Always debating.

When Sarah lived in Chicago, Patrick happened to be there for law school. Two people from completely different parts of my life in the same city. I remember how much that warmed my heart.

I was in law school when he came to my parents' house to tell me about the amazing girl he met. He was in love. I was so happy for him as I had never seen him like this. He asked for my advice on rings. When he finally bought it, he couldn't wait to show it to me. Then he asked me to be his best man. Without hesitation, I said yes.

During the wedding planning Patrick asked if I wanted to wear some version of a bridesmaid dress or whether I wanted something else. I chose something else. A black tuxedo style suit. At the rehearsal he and I were in the church near the altar goofing around. We couldn't help ourselves as that's just how we were. As Patrick's fiancée was making her way to the back of the church to walk up the aisle, the priest yelled at us and told us to get it together.

It's strange, whenever any of my girlfriends were in serious relationships, I always felt threatened. I could feel that our relationship was going to change. With Patrick, I thought it would be different.

But the moment he said "I do," something shifted. Years earlier we argued about whether men and women could really be just friends. I said yes. He said eventually someone would always feel more.

Standing in that church on his wedding day, I finally understood what he meant. He didn't love me differently. He loved someone else first.

I started to pull back. Respecting his marriage is what I was doing. There were fewer calls, longer gaps of time passing. Months became years.

Being respectful was my excuse. But that was bullshit. I questioned where I fit in his life anymore, and instead of staying to find out, I left.

Again.

The last time I saw Patrick was at my dad's funeral.

Standing in the funeral home by my dad's casket, greeting everyone who came to pay their respects was exhausting.

"Thank you for coming." I sounded like a broken record.

"He was a great man and will be missed," people repeated.

Over and over.

There was a lull in visitors and I looked up to see Patrick walk in. He gave me a smile that warmed my heart and crushed my soul at the same time. He hugged me. He showed up for me in the worst moment of my life.

I wanted to grab his hand and run to the diner with him. Rewind time. Go fight like hell over the color of the sun. Anything to go back to the old versions of us.

All I had time for was to say, "It's so good to see you. Thank you so much for coming." That was the last time I saw him.

One of the things that hurt so much about Patrick was that just a few weeks before my aunt emailed me his obituary, he popped into my head. Out of nowhere. I hadn't thought about him in years. I remember thinking I should call him. One of these days.

But who was I kidding? Calling meant admitting I missed him. That I wanted him back in my life. But I had left. I didn't call. I couldn't admit that I needed my old friend back in my life.

And now he was dead.

I was too scared to risk rejection. I couldn't bear to hear him say that it had been too long or worse, that he wouldn't answer. But here's the thing. He wouldn't have said or done either. I hadn't talked to him in years and he showed up for me at my dad's funeral. He showed up for me when I hadn't for him.

I learned something when my dad was dying. Time runs out. You can make all of the plans for the future, but one day you may be told your future is now. I learned about not waiting or walking away from people that matter. I thought I had learned it with Sarah.

The urgency that you recognize in those precious final moments fades. Bad habits don't. The joke's on me. You don't always have time. Sometimes one of these days becomes never.

Patrick is gone. I don't get to fix our relationship. I'll never be able to tell him how much I missed him or how sorry I am for leaving. I won't ever know who we became as adults who stayed.

But it wasn't just Patrick I walked away from. It turns out, I've spent my whole life looking for people I belong with, and somehow convincing myself I'll never find them.

Chapter 10: *Still Looking*

I have lived in six states and in Italy. I lived in our Nation's Capital during pivotal moments like the unveiling of the AIDS quilt along the national mall and the election of our nation's first black president. I experienced living in a foreign country where I had a decent understanding of the language but immersed myself in the culture. I moved to the suburbs in the South, where I adjusted to happy hour specials that didn't involve liquor because of the laws and stores that didn't open until after church on Sundays. I lived across the country in the Pacific Northwest where "damp" took on a whole new meaning. And now I am in the west, where sometimes I feel more out of place than I ever have before.

In each place, I met and made friends. Some from work, others from hobbies like yoga, and now, moms of kids my daughter's age. I'm an extrovert, so meeting and talking with people is never my problem. Letting people in? That's where I draw the line.

Ever since those summers at Woodland Heights pool, I've had this image of female friendship that I've quietly yearned for. A group of women the same age who are there for each other through thick and thin. Your ride or dies. The ones you escape with for girls' trips.

The girls from the pool are all still friends, but I am not included in that group anymore. I stay in contact with a few via text or Facebook, but when I see pictures of them getting together annually, I feel a small, familiar twinge of jealousy. They are still a tribe. After all these years, they're still showing up for one another in the moments that mark a life. Weddings, kids, the loss of parents. They're still together and choosing each other.

But the girls did something that shocked me and made me question myself all over again. A week after my mom passed, I got a package in the mail. It was a beautiful wind chime engraved with my mom's name and a memorial message. The card attached said, "We have such wonderful memories of your mom from when we were kids, especially sleepovers at your house. She was always so good to us." It was from the girls at Woodland Heights pool. All of them except Lauren.

Maybe I was wrong all of those years ago. I assumed I never quite fit in and I chose to keep a distance. What if they didn't see me that way at all and the reason they never reached out was because of me, not them? Maybe they thought I didn't want to keep up the friendships. Those girls are still together. And I'm not. But whose choice was that, really?

I never stayed close with anyone from high school except Amy. We'd been friends since we were kids. She's one year younger, but we went to grade school, high school, and even college together. Moving through life side by side. We spent part of our single lives going out in DC, learning to be adults and discovering who we were.

One time in our mid-20s, we decided to take a trip to Paris together. I had been there before, once with Mark, and this was her first time. Amy is a planner, and I am not. She came prepared, with her highlighted Rick Steves book, ensuring we had everything mapped out for where to eat and what to see. I was responsible for booking our hotel.

Once we landed, we took a cab to our hotel and I remember a sense of deja vu as the driver headed into a neighborhood I recognized. I had been in this area of Paris before with Mark. As the cab slowed upon arriving at our hotel, I sat there frozen. This is the same hotel where I stayed with Mark and it was a bit of a dump. How could I have been so stupid that I didn't remember this? This is why I don't do the planning.

Amy loves art and The Louvre was high on her list of things to see in Paris. Museums aren't my thing. I know it sounds crazy, but I have been to Paris a few times and have yet to go there. While Amy planned her museum route, I mapped out shopping districts. Clothes, shoes, jewelry. That's the art I love.

Amy and I are opposite in many ways. But that's what makes our friendship so special. We appreciate how different we are and love each other all the more for it. I pushed her away when I was with Ryan, but I didn't have to apologize like I did with Sarah.

Amy and I have a unique friendship. We can go long stretches without talking and pick up like we just spoke yesterday. We've been there for each other for the big moments and small ones. She married years before I did. Now we live far apart, but we've stayed close anyway. Amy's the exception, not the rule.

When I wasn't going to happy hour with the guys from work, I was trying to build friendships with the women. Some of those connections lasted. Others fizzled the moment one of us changed jobs.

One constant in my professional life was how easily I connected with younger women. Often I was their boss, always trying to walk the thin line between professionalism and something deeper. There was mentorship and the beginnings of friendship. I wanted to help them grow. I felt pulled toward them in a way that went beyond the job. But age always loomed between us, the same invisible barrier I'd felt with the girls from the pool.

I enjoyed spending time with these women outside of work, though I was always aware I was the older friend. The one who didn't catch the jokes or understand the references. There's a particular kind of humbling moment when you say something like, "Talk to me, Goose," only to be met with blank stares. "Huh? Who is Goose?" So I slowly retreated.

But women my age? That's where I fail. I've met some wonderful moms in the neighborhood. They invite me to wine nights and playdates for the kids. Sometimes I say yes, then cancel. But when I do show up, I spend the whole time feeling like I don't measure up or feeling like we just don't have much in common.

Who has the better career? Whose kids are thriving? Who seems more put-together? The questions just keep coming. I'm measuring myself against them before they even speak. It's exhausting so I just keep my distance.

I remember so many people telling me to wait until Mia was in school and then I would meet other mom friends. We would share that common experience of having kids the same age but even that hasn't been easy.

I was standing in the pickup line at school one afternoon in May. A group of moms stood a few feet away, the same cluster that always formed. I knew them because our kids were in the same class. But I wasn't part of the circle.

They were talking about summer camps. Specifically, judging parents who use summer camps. "I just don't understand putting your kid in camp all summer," one of them said. "Like, don't you want to spend time with them?"

Another mom nodded. "We're doing two weeks max. The rest is just being together. Going to the pool, doing things around the area, whatever."

"Some people just aren't really present with their kids."

I stood there pretending to look at my phone.

Then one of them turned to me. "What's Mia doing this summer?"

I answered honestly. "She's got camps almost every week. We both work full time."

The mom smiled. You know that kind that says oh, I see.

"That's great. I'm sure she'll have fun."

Then she turned back to the group. They kept talking about their summers and all the things they wanted to do with their kids.

I returned to my phone and stood there waiting for Mia to come out.

I wasn't jealous of them. I never wanted to be a stay-at-home mom. I'd worked too hard to build a career to give it up. But standing there, I felt it again. The impossible choice society hands to mothers. You can have a career but you'll be judged for not being present enough. You can stay home but you'll lose yourself. Either way, you lose.

I wanted Mia to see that she could do both. That work didn't make me less present or less loving. But how could I show her that when every interaction with these moms felt like proof I was doing it wrong?

When Mia came running out, I took her hand and walked to the car quickly. I didn't look back.

That night I told Irwin about it. "They were judging me."

"So what? We both work. Mia loves camp. Who cares what they think?"

"I care. Because Mia's watching. I want her to know she can have both. But it's like society won't let you. I'm either a bad mom for working or I'm giving up everything to prove that I care about my daughter. It's bullshit."

He didn't have an answer. Neither did I.

Some of the women I've truly let in are older than me by 16 years. Nancy, my next-door neighbor in Seattle, and Diane, my neighbor here, and Lynn, a friend from California. All these women are in their 60s. With them, I can be honest. I don't have to perform. I'm not comparing my life to theirs or worrying about being judged.

Diane's husband had cancer and his decline was quick. One month he was fine, the next month he wasn't.

I sat with her at the hospital and made sure she ate during our long days there. I sat with her husband when she needed a break and helped translate what the doctors were saying. I'd worked in cancer and had been through this with my dad so I knew the questions to ask.

One afternoon she called and her voice was shaking. "Can you help me get him to the car? I need to take him to the ER."

Irwin and I ran over immediately. When I saw him, I knew. He looked like my dad had looked those last few weeks. Weak and struggling to walk.

"I'll go with you," I said, and climbed in the back seat. Irwin followed in his car.

At the ER the docs said he needed emergency surgery and it was risky. They weren't sure he'd make it.

I saw the panic in her eyes and I knew that fear. I felt it signing DNR papers for my dad. I'd felt it watching my mom die alone.

I grabbed her hand and she squeezed back hard.

That was the moment I understood what it meant to actually show up for someone. Not school pickup small talk or "we should get coffee sometime" that never happens. Real friendship, the kind that shows up when everything's falling apart.

He made it through the surgery but he died a few weeks later.

I stayed with her through it all, especially those weeks after when everyone else went back to their lives and she was left alone. People did that to me and that pain runs deep. The pain when you know your life is irrevocably changed and it's too uncomfortable for others. They don't know what to say or how to act so they just disappear.

Diane and I bonded in grief. Not in bullshit conversations about summer camps but in the kind of pain that strips everything else away.

After he died, I thought about those moms at pickup judging me for working and I realized I don't want friends who make me feel like shit about my choices. I want friends who show up when it's hard. Friends who make you feel safe and chosen.

Diane, Nancy and Lynn are in their 60s. We're not supposed to fit but we do. Because real friendship isn't about having the same schedule or being at the same life stage. It's about showing up.

That's what I want Mia to see.

It's not that I can't make friends. I just struggle to open up to some women. Just like my mom. She died with one friend. If she had a funeral, there wouldn't have been a tribe of women showing up. She'd pushed them all away, all except one. I watched her die alone and told myself I'd never do that.

Here's the contradiction I've had to sit with. I pushed away the people who loved me most when I needed them, like Sarah and Amy. I'd kept them at arm's length the whole time I was with Ryan. They were the ones who knew me best and would be able to tell something was wrong so I cut them out before they could figure it out. I chose him over everyone and called it loyalty when really it was shame.

So I understand why some people have seen me as guarded, maybe even cold. I can see how it looked from the outside.

But here's what's also true. For the people I let in, when I'm in a place to actually show up, I show up completely and without question.

I was in that hospital waiting room with Diane because there was nowhere else I would have been. I answered every 2am call that ever came. I showed up at funerals, sat in waiting rooms, and brought food when someone couldn't get off the couch. I don't disappear when things get hard.

I'm not someone who does things halfway. When you're in my circle and I'm in my right mind, you're in it for good.

The problem was never loyalty. It was letting people get close enough to know they could call. And making sure I was in good enough shape to answer.

But here I am, approaching my 50s, settled in a place for the long haul, and I'm still looking for my people. I am still keeping everyone at a safe distance.

I understand what I'm doing now. I see myself comparing and measuring against others. I know that I walk away before anyone can walk away from me. I see it all so clearly. But recognizing it and fixing it aren't the same thing.

I've spent my whole life telling myself I was better off alone. I always believed needing people was a weakness. If I left first, no one could hurt me.

But I wasn't always alone. Once, I stopped running long enough to let someone in. That changed everything.

Part Four:

What's Real

Chapter 11: *The One Who Chose You*

Moving to Raleigh just 10 months after my dad died was another massive change layered onto a year that already felt relentless. I bought my first house and left DC after nearly 15 years in a place I had come to love almost as much as my hometown.

I arrived in North Carolina in late May, stepping into a new leadership role at work, while learning how to adjust to life in the South. I was navigating home ownership for the first time, furnishing a space far larger than the 700 square feet I had lived in for years, adjusting to the slower pace of the South, and trading the wail of sirens for the nightly chorus of frogs in the pond behind my house. Everything was new, and I was more unsettled than I wanted to admit.

It was an adjustment, without question, but what other choice did I really have, having already agreed to move with my boss from DC?

I didn't know a single person in Raleigh. The only familiar things in my life were my boss from DC, who had moved a few months before me, and Scooby. My office was near his and was situated among some of the senior leadership of the cancer center. In July, only a few short months after I arrived, one of the VPs told me I needed to meet with a guy on her team named Irwin. He could help with a project that we brought with us from DC.

We met later that week. He was Chinese-American, good-looking, kind, and really smart. We talked through the work, he offered smart suggestions, and when he left, I remember thinking he seemed like such a great guy. It was nice to meet someone close to my age, but I didn't think much of it beyond that.

DC had trained me to expect young professionals everywhere. There's always a happy hour a stone's throw away. Gathering after work for a drink is a ritual in DC. It's where people network and mostly talk about themselves. Raleigh felt like another planet. My colleagues went home to their spouses and kids. And when five o'clock came, there were no plans to head out to a patio for a drink. There were liquor laws prohibiting alcohol at happy hour. It felt like the Twilight Zone.

Taking pity on me, the same VP invited me to a Durham Bulls game with her team. She had a whole department under her. I didn't. It was just me and my boss from DC. I needed to start saying yes. As much as I loved being home with Scooby, I was in my early 30s, new to the South, and 10 months out from my dad's death. I couldn't afford to disappear into my house.

The Raleigh-Durham sports scene was college teams and Durham Bulls, the minor league club made famous by the 80s movie. Walking into that stadium and seeing the giant bull sign, it hit me. This was my life now.

I found the section that had been reserved and took a seat. A few innings in, Irwin showed up and sat in the empty seat next to me. He looked like he'd come straight from the gym wearing a ratty T-shirt, workout shorts, and the ugliest white sneakers I'd ever seen. I gave him shit about his outfit and joked that he looked like he'd rolled off the basketball court to a work event. He laughed, and then said, "As a matter of fact, I did just come from a basketball game." In DC, appearances mattered, but Irwin's casual confidence threw me. I left that night surprised by how much fun I'd had.

The next day he emailed me. Not about work. And that was it. We started writing back and forth, long, easy emails that stretched over weeks. I found myself waiting for them and smiling when one hit my inbox.

In August, he asked me to dinner. It was a date, and I was nervous. I remember going shopping and I bought an orange sleeveless crepe top, a departure from my usual DC black and navy. We met at an Italian restaurant and stayed for hours. Somewhere between pasta and a second glass of wine, my birthday came up.

When I told him my birthday, he froze. "No way" was his response. Then he laughed and pulled out his license.

Same day. Same year. WTF!

We hugged in the parking lot and made plans for the weekend. He had tickets for a charity golf tournament. I hate golf but I didn't care. We spent the day together, then went to lunch, and when we realized there was a Durham Bulls game that night, neither of us wanted it to end. We went home to change and met back at the stadium.

The night ended, and still, no kiss.

This was turning out to be so different from any man I had dated before. Everything moved more slowly, more intentionally. It was already beginning to feel real, meaningful, different in a way I hadn't known I was missing.

In the past, sex often followed quickly after meeting someone. Looking back, I think I felt like if I didn't give it up quickly, the guy would leave. Turns out, that's the theory I should have tested. I could have eliminated quite a bit of heartache.

I remembered a friend once telling me I needed to make a man earn it. At the time, I dismissed her advice entirely. What did she know about being single? She'd been married since her mid-20s, with her husband since college. Still, standing there in that unfamiliar slowness, I began to wonder if she'd understood something I hadn't yet learned.

As our birthday approached, we made plans for a celebratory dinner at one of the fanciest restaurants in the area. I bought a silk, backless animal-print dress, something that made me feel pretty and was a bit out of my comfort zone, not like the black

A-line dresses that were part of my wardrobe. This night felt different, and I wanted to mark it that way.

Irwin wore a suit. When we arrived, the restaurant glowed with low, romantic lighting, classical music floating softly through the room. It was the kind of place with multiple courses and tiny palate cleansers served on delicate spoons between each dish.

At some point in the evening, the conversation shifted. We began talking about our future, tentatively at first, then more directly. We hinted at marriage. The idea should have felt absurd, but instead it made a quiet kind of sense.

We had only been seeing each other for a few months, but we were both 35. We had lived full lives before we met. He had lost his father too. We knew grief and pain. We had both survived toxic, emotionally abusive relationships. We had lost ourselves and rebuilt. I had endured law school; he had spent six grueling years earning his PhD.

We weren't rushing toward something unknown. We were recognizing something familiar. As the conversation continued I noticed something profound. The music playing was no longer classical, but rather jazz. The sound of a trumpet solo filled the air. Tears began to well in my eyes. My dad was a magnificent trumpet player. I looked at Irwin, holding back tears, and said, "I think my dad approves of you." Our conversation moved on to something else and so did the music. It returned back to classical.

This was the first and only sign I received from my dad after he died.

I was riding the high from our birthday celebration for about three days. Then the panic set in. This was too good to be true. We had that same birthday. We could talk for hours like no time had passed. He actually wanted to get to know me, not just sleep with me. It was real in a way nothing else had ever been.

I was terrified. Every man before him had proven the same thing. I wasn't the girl men kept. Mark didn't want me. Drew didn't want me. Ryan nearly destroyed me. The pattern was clear. So why would Irwin be different?

I started looking for reasons to walk away. Our cultures were too different, him being Asian and me Italian. We worked together. It was moving too fast. I could end it now before I got in too deep, before he could hurt me.

But I didn't. I don't know why. Maybe I was tired of running and tired of being alone. Or maybe my dad was right and was telling me not to let this guy go.

So I stayed and I waited for the other shoe to drop. It never did.

Irwin and I were married 11 months later.

Our wedding was small, around 65 people. We paid for it ourselves so we made it ours. No expectations of parents or what tradition says we should do. Since most people were coming from out of town, we hosted everyone at our house Friday night. We had NC BBQ catered. It was a chance for both sides to meet before the wedding. Irwin's Chinese family mixing with my loud Italian relatives. I wasn't sure how it would go, but it worked.

The wedding itself was non-traditional. My dad was gone so I walked down the aisle with Scooby. He wore a red bow tie. That and the red accents in my hair piece and belt were a nod to Irwin's Chinese heritage.

We didn't get married in a church. I'd already left the Catholic Church by then but even if I hadn't, they wouldn't have married us. Irwin wasn't religious, nor was he baptized. Another judgment from the Church I wouldn't stand for. So we found a venue that let us create our ceremony, the way we wanted it.

We did family-style meals because that married both our cultures. Chinese and Italian families both understand that food is love, that sharing a meal together matters. We performed a traditional Chinese tea ceremony, serving tea to the family elders. Irwin's mom, my mom. Some aunts and uncles. It was a way to honor his heritage and show respect.

And to honor my heritage, we had a traditional Pittsburgh cookie table. Hundreds of cookies baked by my grandmother and brought to North Carolina by my cousins. Pizzelles, biscotti, nut rolls, lady locks. People not from Pittsburgh had never seen anything like it. Cookie tables aren't just dessert. They're a tradition for Italian Pittsburgh weddings.

We hired a jazz quartet to honor my dad and his love of jazz and the trumpet. When they played during dinner, I closed my eyes and imagined him there. He would have loved this. He would have loved Irwin.

Standing at the altar with Irwin, it clicked. For the first time in my life, I wasn't wondering if this would last. I wasn't looking for reasons to leave. I never thought once about him changing his mind.

He'd chosen me. And I'd chosen him back.

The wedding wasn't what my parents would have wanted. It wasn't in a church. My dad wasn't there to walk me down the aisle. My mom sat in the front row looking lost without him. But it was ours. Irwin and me. We chose how to blend our families and our cultures, creating something new.

For someone who spent her whole life running before she could be left, standing there saying "I do" felt like the biggest risk I'd ever taken.

He was the first who made me wait. Made me believe I was worth the effort. Worth choosing. My mom was married a month after she turned 22. Still a baby. She didn't experience adulthood the way we did. We explored the world. We made our mistakes and ended up finding our way. And now we know what we're choosing and why.

I thought finding Irwin would be the final piece. That I'd figured it all out. But then I became a mother. And I started to understand what I'd been carrying all along.

Chapter 12: *When You Choose Yourself*

Looking back, when I was asked what I wanted to be when I grew up, my answer was always doctor. I don't remember whether I ever played pretend doctor with my stuffed animals. I don't remember if I had some profound life-changing encounter with one of my doctors that made me think, I want to do that when I grow up. I think in large part it had to do with my parents and their influence.

I did science fairs and won first place at the state level. I worked in a lab in high school. Everything I did pointed toward medicine. I was working toward the future I had always known. And then, right before college, I had an epiphany.

I didn't actually want to be a doctor.

I liked healthcare, but I had zero tolerance for blood or bodily fluids. None. Suddenly, the plan I'd been following for years collapsed. I was set to be a biology major, and there was no universe in which my parents were going to be okay with me showing up undeclared.

So the week before school started, I opened the course catalog. Yes, it was an actual book because it was the 90s. I closed my eyes, flipped the pages, and dropped my finger. I promised myself I would stick with whatever it landed on.

Philosophy. What the hell does one do with that?

My parents looked at me like I'd just announced I was majoring in unemployment.

After a few minutes my dad said, "Well…the only thing you can really do with that is go to law school."

My mom added that I argued like Judge Judy, which apparently meant I was a future attorney. And just like that, law school became the plan.

I actually loved law school. I even liked studying for the Bar, which is something no one admits out loud. Practicing law, though? That was awful. I made it one year before I knew, without a shadow of a doubt, that this was not my life.

I wanted to work in a hospital, though I had no idea how that would happen. I kept it to myself. If I said it out loud too soon, my parents would have tried to talk me back into a life that I knew I didn't want. I only told them after I'd been offered a job managing a department at a children's hospital. By then, the decision was made. I wasn't leaving law. I had already left.

To say they were pissed is an understatement. I heard, "what a waste of money on your education," "why would you throw your career away," and my dad, who was known to be even-tempered, hung up on me right after he said, "If you do this, I can't support it."

I remember staring at my phone after, stunned by the quiet. I expected that reaction from my mom, but not my dad. And that stung.

I didn't call my parents back and they didn't call me. A week went by and I was still hurt. But I wasn't backing down and I definitely wasn't sharing the story about being taken advantage of by a lawyer at my firm.

This was long before the Me Too movement and I carried a lot of shame and guilt. If I told them what happened, they'd ask questions. And the answers would damn me. I was drinking that night. He was married. I went to a bar with him alone.

I could already hear them. "What did you expect would happen?" "Why would you put yourself in that position?" "You should have known better."

They would have been disappointed in me, and I couldn't handle that on top of everything else.

When I finally called, my mom answered. She was still angry, but she let me talk. I told them both this was happening whether they liked it or not. That I'd rather be happy than successful by their definition.

My dad got on the phone. He didn't apologize for hanging up. But he said, "If this is what you're doing, then do it right."

I was a spokesperson for my job at the children's hospital. Whenever I made a TV appearance on CNN, my dad always recorded the segment. After he died, I was looking for some insurance paperwork in his office. He had a manilla folder for everything. Organization was his love language. While sifting through the folders, I found one labeled *Chrissy Media*. I pulled out the folder and opened it up. Inside was a copy of every article I had been interviewed for or quoted in. USA Today. NY Times. NPR. Washington Post. He had copies of every single one. He'd been keeping them the whole time. I know he was proud of my career and when I found that folder, it sealed any doubts I had about his feelings, but I wish I had truly known how proud he was while he was alive.

My mom loved telling people I was an attorney. She made it known anytime people asked her how I was doing in DC. Even years after I quit, she'd introduce me that way. Every birthday card she sent was addressed with Esq following my name, like she couldn't let it go.

It wasn't about me being happy. It was about what she could tell people. Having a daughter who was a lawyer looked good. Having a daughter who quit to work in healthcare? That required an explanation.

After leaving the children's hospital, I began working in cancer. Having lost my aunt to it while I was in law school, I felt a deep need to work in an area that I had such an intimate connection with. I went on to work at several prestigious cancer centers across the country, and in many ways it was the most meaningful work I've ever done. I met care teams who gave everything they had to their patients. People who stayed late, bent rules, made miracles out of logistics.

After we were married, Irwin and I moved to Seattle and I continued my career in cancer. When I was pregnant, I was leading a brain tumor center, and that nearly broke me. I had already lost my dad, and years later, I was still burying that grief, still functioning on the outside while carrying it everywhere inside. But there was something uniquely brutal about watching people my own age, already parents, die from glioblastoma, a diagnosis that almost always ends the same way.

I was the administrator at the center. While I wasn't directly involved in patient care, I oversaw the clinic. The front desk staff, who scheduled appointments. The nurses, who helped families through chemo. The social workers, who met with patients and their families. The providers, who had the impossible job of helping patients and families navigate one of the ugliest cancer diagnoses.

One patient stayed with me. He was in his late 30s with a wife and a three-year-old daughter and had been diagnosed with glioblastoma. The tumor was causing personality changes, and he was angry, lashing out at everyone. It's an unfortunate side effect of certain tumor locations. The brain doesn't just control your body. It controls who you are.

His wife would come to appointments exhausted and terrified. The staff would tell me about the conversations. How he'd been sweet before the diagnosis and now he couldn't control his rage. How their daughter was scared of him. His wife was so torn because she didn't know how much longer she could keep him at home.

The social worker met with the wife separately one afternoon and when she came out of that meeting, she looked wrecked. I asked if she was okay. She wasn't. They were talking about removing him from the home because they were afraid he would harm himself or worse, his wife or daughter.

"He has a three-year-old," the social worker said to me, tears in her eyes.

"She's not going to remember him like this, right? She'll remember him before?"

I didn't have an answer.

I watched the toll it took on the staff. The nurses, who had to explain to the wife why her husband couldn't control his anger. The schedulers, who heard her crying on the phone trying to get him to another appointment. The social worker, trying to help a family navigate an impossible situation. And the providers, trying to keep the patient on track with treatment, knowing it was an unwinnable fight, but just trying to give him more time.

It was heartbreaking, and I was pregnant.

This patient was in his late 30s and his daughter was three. I was just a few years older and my daughter would be born in a few months.

I started thinking about it constantly. What if that was Irwin? What if that was me? What if our daughter was three and I was dying and couldn't control who I was becoming? I couldn't stop worrying.

Every ache I thought was cancer. Every headache convinced me I had a tumor. I'd wake up in the middle of the night and lie there thinking about symptoms.

My back hurt. The rational thought that my back hurt because I was pregnant wasn't even a possibility. It had to be cancer.

My shoulder was stiff. Was that a sign? I Googled everything. I convinced myself I was dying. I was paralyzed with fear that I was going to get cancer and leave my child without a mother.

One afternoon I was standing in the hallway and I saw the patient's wife walking out with their daughter. The little girl was holding her mom's hand and looking back toward the exam room where her dad was. She looked so confused and scared.

I went into my office and closed the door. I sat at my desk and couldn't breathe. What if that was my daughter? My family?

I'd worked in cancer for years. Patients dying was part of the job. Years before, when I was running a pancreatic cancer program, there was a woman in her 30s who was pregnant with pancreatic cancer. I sat in meetings about when to start chemo, what to do if the mother deteriorated. At the time, kids weren't even on my radar. I could sit in those meetings and stay professional. I could compartmentalize.

But now, I was pregnant. And I couldn't do it anymore. I'd never had something to lose like this.

When my dad was dying, I'd been strong. I'd signed the DNR. I'd planned the funeral. I ate nails for breakfast and kept going. But watching this man in his late 30s with a three-year-old daughter, the weight of it hit me. I wasn't strong. I was terrified.

I couldn't do this job anymore. Not while every patient felt like a mirror showing me my worst fear.

I gave birth to Mia just shy of my 40th birthday.

I was supposed to go back to work after three months. I'd told myself I would be fine. I willed myself to believe the anxiety would settle once she was here and real and safe.

But I couldn't do it. I couldn't walk back into that clinic knowing what I knew. There was no way I could watch more families falling apart while I left my daughter at daycare wondering if that would be us one day.

I told Irwin I couldn't go back. He was so supportive. He'd watched me spiral for months.

"So don't," he said. "We'll figure it out."

I didn't go back. I left a career I'd been good at, one that was personal. But I knew I couldn't survive watching other people's families break while trying to protect my own.

That's what grief does. It doesn't just take the people you love. It takes your ability to imagine a future where you're safe.

I left my career after Mia was born, and I knew quickly that staying home full-time wasn't for me. I took a few metalsmithing classes, almost on a whim, and fell in love. In my first class, I made a simple sterling silver pendant, setting a turquoise stone Irwin had picked up for me on one of his trips. The moment I slid the chain through the bail and put it on, something clicked. I could do this. I could make jewelry.

We moved to Colorado not long after, and our new house had space for a small studio. I set up my bench and my tools, and got to work.

I had always loved fashion and jewelry. I still own the first piece I ever bought with my own money, a custom sterling ring with a pink sapphire and two tanzanites from a small artisan shop in Pittsburgh. Years later, after I launched my business, that same jeweler found my work online and began complimenting me on my designs. It felt surreal, like a subtle blessing from a former version of myself.

Six months after that first class, I formed my LLC. Three months after that, I was showing my work in New York City. I didn't pay myself for five years, but I had never felt more fulfilled. I had never studied art or been encouraged to be creative, but once I found it, I loved both the making and business.

At shows, I saw women light up when a piece spoke to them. They stood a little taller and gave off an air of confidence. Those moments made every long, solitary hour at the bench worth it.

My mom saw my work before she died. I used to text her photos of new designs. She never hid her opinions. When she hated something, I secretly knew I was onto something.

After she died, a design came to me that felt like her. A heavy sterling cuff, oxidized black, hammered into uneven waves. In one dip, I set a small turquoise stone in 18k gold. I named the piece after her. The waves were our relationship. The turquoise in gold was the beauty that existed even inside the hard parts.

Two women bought that bracelet after hearing its story. Each had her own complicated history with her mother. Both told me it gave them comfort. I wasn't just making jewelry anymore. It was about connection.

If you ask my daughter what she wants to be when she grows up, her answer is unwavering. An artist. And I get it now. I was a jewelry artist and know how it feels to create something beautiful out of nothing.

Mia loves to draw and, while I may sound biased, she's damn good at it. I see how much pride she takes in her work and she is a bit of a perfectionist like me. But admittedly this scares me.

I know how hard it can be to make a living as an artist. I worked alongside other artists for years when I had my jewelry business and it can be a slog. But I also know how it felt to make my own career decisions, away from the influence of my parents. It was terrifying but also the most rewarding decision I made. I bet on myself and I won.

I had to close my business after five years because of a nagging shoulder injury that required surgery. Years of tennis and the repetitive motions of handcrafting jewelry did me in, and as I approached 50, I didn't want to live with chronic pain for the rest of my life.

Looking back, I wonder if I've been doing the same thing with my career that I did with friendships. Leaving before things could fail. I left law before I could fail at it. I closed the jewelry business because of my shoulder, sure, but also because it was getting bigger and scarier. What if I had someone else make pieces that I designed and it was a failure? What if people stopped buying? What if I would never be able to take a salary?

It's the same instinct. Walk away before you can be left. Quit before you can be fired. Close the business before it can close on you.

But with Mia, I can't do that. I can't protect her from failure by telling her not to try. I have to let her choose, even if it scares me. Even if she fails. I can support her dreams and empower her to bet on herself the way I did. I can show her that choosing what you love over what's safe is worth it.

But there's one thing I can't teach her how to navigate. One thing I can't protect her from, no matter how much I want to. The world won't just see her as an artist. They'll see her as other. And I have no idea how to prepare her for that.

Chapter 13: *When She's the Other*

I thought marrying Irwin would finally mean I belonged somewhere. I'd found my person so that should have been enough. What I didn't expect was that marrying him would make me feel like an outsider in my own family.

I grew up thinking everyone lived like we did. White. Catholic. Middle class. Don't get me wrong, there was diversity in Pittsburgh, but it was defined by geography. The Hill District was where Black families lived. Bloomfield was Little Italy. Squirrel Hill was Jewish. Polish Hill was Polish. I grew up in a place where people were defined as others based on where they lived and where they were from.

Pittsburgh is known for its friendliness and the warmth of its people. People would give you the shirt off their back or invite you into their home for food if you were in need. But there was real structural segregation underneath all that friendliness.

I am not going to pretend I didn't hear racist comments growing up. Times were different then, and while that doesn't excuse the behavior, it does make me understand the culture in which I grew up and vow to do better. To be more open and not judge.

When I moved to DC, I was a minority in the city. And that taught me a lot about how I wanted to move through the world as an adult. I didn't see color or ethnicity when it came to men. I guess it makes sense that I ended up in an interracial marriage, but growing up in Western Pennsylvania, I'm an exception to the norm.

When my mom met one of my boyfriends who was black, she told me to "never tell my father that we were together." When I would tell her if I was hanging out with Miguel, I would get "why are you wasting your time with *these* boys?" I think my mom always suspected I would marry outside of my race based on my dating history, but when I did, I don't think I was fully prepared for some of the comments I received.

Irwin and I got engaged in Pittsburgh, on Father's Day weekend. He wanted to make it special, knowing how hard it had been for me since my dad passed. We celebrated with my dad's side of the family. My grandmother, aunts, uncles, and a few cousins all came. This was the first time any of them would meet Irwin in person.

At 92, my grandmother made a feast of homemade pasta, meatballs, sausage, antipasto, and homemade bread. The table was full. It was reminiscent of the Sunday dinners I grew up with, and I was thrilled Irwin got a taste of my childhood.

The table was loud. Everyone talking over each other, passing dishes, refilling wine glasses. My uncle asked Irwin about his work. A cousin wanted to know how we met. Conversation was flowing and everyone seemed excited to get to know him.

"Irwin," my grandmother said, reaching for the pasta bowl. "You're Oriental, right?"

The table went quiet for a second. I felt my face get hot.

"Chinese," I said quickly. "His family is Chinese."

"Were you born there?"

"My parents were born in China and grew up in Taiwan, and I was born in California," Irwin said evenly.

One of my aunts chimed in. "When I went to Asia, I didn't eat a lot. I wasn't sure what anything was and I didn't want to eat dog. I know some places do that over there."

There was a faint laughter around the table. My grandmother just kept serving food like nothing happened.

I opened my mouth to say something but nothing came out. My throat felt tight. I looked at Irwin. His face was neutral but I could see it in his eyes.

"That's not…" I started with a little bite in my tone.

Irwin just gave me a look that said *let it go*.

My uncle changed the subject to ask about our work again. Someone else asked about our wedding plans. The conversation moved on.

But I sat there, my face burning, replaying it in my head. Did my family really just say Oriental and reference eating dog to my fiancé? What a shit show.

To them, this was just conversation. They didn't mean anything by it.

But it wasn't nothing.

When we left, I couldn't apologize fast enough. "I'm so sorry. I didn't know they'd say that. I should have…"

"It's okay," he said.

"It's not okay. That was…"

"I know. It is what it is."

I knew none of it was fine. He let it go because he didn't want to make things harder for me. But I was mortified that my family believed these things and felt that they were appropriate to say.

I sat at that table, between my future husband and my family, and felt the gap widen. They weren't trying to be hurtful. My grandmother lived in an Italian immigrant community outside of the city where everyone looked like her. Oriental was the word people used then. She didn't know it was outdated or offensive. The dog comment? That was ignorance, not cruelty. It was something someone probably joked about that she never questioned.

But Irwin still heard it and I still sat there, frozen.

I wasn't angry at them. I was heartbroken. At that moment, I understood that my family lives in a different world than I do. I can't bring them into mine any more than I can go back to theirs.

It's not that they are bad people. They just couldn't see beyond what they knew. And that meant I was standing in the middle, not quite belonging to either side anymore.

During Covid, I called my mom to talk about how scared I was for Mia and Irwin. Hate crimes against Asian Americans were spiking. I was terrified every time they left the house.

"Mia is white," my mom said. "What are you talking about?"

"She's half Asian, Mom. She—"

"You're making a bigger deal out of this than it is," she interrupted.

I tried to argue that she was mixed race, but my mom didn't want to hear it. In her mind, despite distinctive Asian features, Mia was white and I was being dramatic.

This was ignorance and white privilege on display from my own family once again. My mom wasn't being cruel. She genuinely didn't see what I was afraid of. To her, Mia looked white enough to be safe. In her world, it made sense.

I was living in a different world now. One where I saw my daughter's Asian features and worried about what that meant for her. I couldn't unsee the way people looked at us, the questions they asked.

My mom and I were looking at the same child and seeing completely different things. That's when I understood that I don't fully belong to the world I came from anymore. We're not living in the same reality.

It wasn't that my mom was hateful, but she couldn't understand. And I couldn't ever make her see it.

I don't blame my family for not understanding. They grew up in neighborhoods where everyone looked the same, talked the same and believed the same things. My grandmother spent 70 years in the same neighborhood. My mom married a man from work and it was my dad's cousin that introduced them.

They are products of their generation, their geography, and their life experiences. They weren't taught to question the language they used or the assumptions they made. I am not saying that makes any of it okay, but it explains it.

What it doesn't explain is the loneliness of standing in the middle. The feeling of loving people who can't quite see your world. And it was a painful realization that my own mother didn't understand it either.

As we reemerged into society after Covid, I quickly learned that this type of ignorance has no bounds.

I participated in a fine art show in Aspen. Irwin and Mia always came along when I did shows around Colorado, helping me set up, and then they went off to enjoy adventures while I worked.

It was common for Mia to spend time at my booth, and usually people loved seeing my daughter with me.

As this woman was looking at my jewelry, Mia had popped into my tent to bring me a snack.

"Is that your daughter?" she asked.

"Yes, this is Mia. Mia, say hi."

"Hi!" Mia said.

"She is so beautiful. Where did you get her?"

"Excuse me?" I know I didn't hear this lady right.

"Your daughter is beautiful. Where did she come from?"

So taken back, I said the first thing that came to mind. "She came out of my vagina."

The woman was mortified, either at the audacity of her own question or at my crass response.

"'I just assumed. She doesn't look anything like you. I'm sorry," she said as she backed out of my tent.

Since that time I have repeatedly been asked the most ridiculous questions.

"Is she adopted?"

"What country did you get her from?"

"Are you her nanny?"

"I adopted my kids from Korea, where did you get her from?" like we shared some secret adoption bond.

These questions don't just sting because they're ignorant. They sting because Mia hears them too.

She was standing right there in Aspen when that woman asked where I "got" her. She hears people ask if she's adopted. She sees the confusion on their faces when they look at us together. And I watch her trying to make sense of it. Why do people think I'm not her mom? Why do they assume she came from somewhere else?

She's starting to see that the world looks at her as not quite belonging to me. She's not quite white enough to be mine without explanation. Her Asian features are strong enough that people don't see me as her mother. She's in between, just like I've always been.

These questions are teaching her the same lesson I learned during my childhood. You're close to the group, but you're not quite in it. You're other.

I don't fit with the white moms who don't have to worry about how the world sees their children. I don't fit with Asian moms who see me as white. I don't fit with my own family who thinks my daughter is white.

And for Mia, she's learning she doesn't quite fit either. Hers for different reasons than mine, but it's the same feeling.

In second grade, Mia came home one day in January and told me about their lesson on Martin Luther King, Jr.

"Mom, have you heard of Martin Luther King, Jr?" she asked.

"Of course, Mia."

"We learned about him today in school. Did you know that he was friends with a white boy in his neighborhood? They played together a lot until they went to school. But the boy's dad didn't like that Martin was black, so he stopped letting his son play with him."

"I didn't know that. That's really sad," I responded.

"Yeah, I don't understand why he would do that. What does it matter that Martin Luther King Jr. was black? That makes no sense to me," she commented as if this should be obvious to everyone.

"Mia, unfortunately not all people think like we do. Some see people of other races and cultures as different and don't always treat them as equal."

When you're seven, school is recess and friends. The lessons are secondary. Mia couldn't get past the fact that these two young boys could no longer play together and be friends because of skin color.

How do I explain this to a kid her age? I shouldn't have to, but with the current state of things in the US, sadly, I have to.

Mia knows she's half Asian, half white, but until that moment, she had no context for what race was and why it mattered to people.

And unfortunately, I don't think it's much different for some adults. I was recently talking with a group of moms about the division that's happening in our country. I told them how I am talking to Mia about everything, keeping certain details vague because she's still a kid, but not shielding her from current events.

The other moms looked at me with horror. They don't follow the news, they said. Their children definitely don't know what's happening in the world. They're choosing to stay uninformed because it's all too much.

I dropped it. At the time, I chalked it up to different parenting styles. But driving home, it hit me. I wasn't angry at them. They weren't being deliberately insensitive. They were just comfortable and felt safe in a world where their kids would never be othered. They didn't need to think about race because it wouldn't touch them in the ways it touches my family.

I feel like I don't fit here either. It is not because they're bad people, because that couldn't be further from the truth. But I feel like our lives are so fundamentally different that we can't even have the same conversations. They get to opt out. I don't. I am living in a reality they'll never have to understand.

A few weeks later, we were watching the Golden Globes together. Teyana Taylor won for best supporting actress and gave an emotional and animated acceptance speech.

"She's being a bit dramatic, isn't she?" Mia said.

I paused the TV. "Do you know how rare it is for Black, Brown and Asian women to win these awards?"

She shook her head.

"In the past, most of the people that won these awards were white. Recently more people of color have been nominated and when they win, it's a big deal. She's not being dramatic. She's celebrating something that doesn't happen often enough. She worked hard and earned this celebration of her art."

"I'm half Asian and half white," Mia said slowly. "What does that mean for me?"

I paused and let her continue because I knew she had more to say.

"Would I not get nominated because I am Asian, or would I get nominated because I am also white?"

I didn't have an answer. And her asking the question at eight years old broke my heart. She's trying to figure out where she fits in knowing she's a mix of both races and cultures.

In the last year she has often asked what it means that she's half Asian and half white. Will people not like her because she's Asian? Will they like her because she's white? I don't know how to respond to her in a way that makes sense for an eight-year-old, but I will keep trying because I owe it to her.

I spent my whole life feeling like I didn't quite belong anywhere. I put myself on the edge of groups, never quite being fully in. And now with my daughter asking the same question I've been asking myself my whole life - where do I fit in? Her question is about race. Mine was about, well, everything else. Maybe they are the same damn question.

I want to tell her she belongs everywhere. That she gets to claim both sides of her heritage. That being mixed is a gift. But I can't lie to her. She's already seen how the world treats her. The questions and assumptions. The woman asking where I "got" her.

So instead I tell her the truth: You're both. You're Italian and Chinese. You're American. You're Mia. And anyone who tries to make you choose doesn't deserve you.

What I don't tell her is that I know what it's like to never quite fit in because I kept myself at the edge of every circle. And my feelings had nothing to do with race.

My family isn't cruel. They are just limited by what they know. The moms aren't bad people. They're comfortable in a way I'll never be again. The gap between their worlds and mine creates that feeling of loneliness. Now Mia might feel this sense of being in between or of not quite fitting anywhere too. But her reasons will be different from mine.

I don't know if I can ever protect her from that, because I've never learned how to bridge that gap myself. All I can do is stand with her in the middle and hope that's enough.

Epilogue: *What I Know Now*

Some women grow up dreaming of being a mother. Some want it so deeply, and it never becomes a reality. Some don't want it and make a heartbreaking choice. Some know, without question, that they never want it at all. Some don't have a loving mother and can't bear to repeat patterns. Some remain open to the idea, believing that if it happens, it happens, and if it doesn't, it doesn't. And some only begin to imagine motherhood when they find a partner and start to envision building a family together.

That last one was me. I was open to the possibility. Open to being known for something beyond my career, open to the chance for something more meaningful, more grounding, and ultimately more rewarding. I was married at 36 and only became receptive to the idea of trying for a child at 39. My husband never pressured me. He knew how I felt when we married. His only comment was that he would regret it if we didn't try.

Time wasn't on our side, so after seeking treatment from a fertility center and with the help of modern medicine and IUI, I delivered my daughter just shy of my 40th birthday. Nothing like entering parenthood at least 10 years after most of your friends.

I don't know whether my apathy towards motherhood came from being so career-focused, from the accumulation of failed relationships and the resignation that marriage might not happen for me, or from wondering whether I had any maternal instincts at all, especially when my own mother was not the most maternal example. No one in my family seemed to believe I would have children, either.

My Italian grandmother, like all older Italian grandmothers, had crocheted a wedding blanket and a baby blanket for me. Knowing her, she probably did this when I was born as I was the only granddaughter and, well, in her mind, my role in life was to be a doting wife and mother. Rather than be proud that I graduated from law school, she said to me shortly after, "I don't know why you went to that school. You should be getting married and having children."

When I reached my early 30s with no prospect of marriage or children, she gave both blankets to me and said, "I made these for you, but since you'll likely never get married or have children, I thought you should have them before I die."

That disbelief didn't end there. When I was finally pregnant at 39, my mother flew from Boston to Seattle when I was eight months along. Despite the photos of my growing belly and the sonogram images I had sent her, she said, "I have to see it with my own two eyes to believe you're actually pregnant." She didn't fly out there to help me nest and get ready. No, she flew out there to see my pregnant belly herself.

I can't fault my mom and grandmother completely. I understand the generational patterns for women my grandmother and mother's age. They often defined themselves primarily as wives, mothers and caretakers. Education wasn't accessible to many of them. There were societal values around appearances and what "people would say." The mentality of don't complain and don't rely on anyone fostered a survival mindset, which was easily passed down to my generation.

Being raised in the 80s defined so much of who I became. The era of feral children and parents who had to be reminded by a television commercial that it was dark outside and maybe they should check if their kids were home. The era of parents who had never been taught the language of emotions, and who passed down the belief that feelings weren't open for discussion, you just dealt with them and moved on. The era of adults telling children to "figure it out."

And we did.

It produced a generation that became independent by necessity. We were emotionally self-contained and resilient, but unsure. Imaginative, unsupervised, and quietly learning how to take care of ourselves long before we were meant to.

And this is where I find myself at a crossroads. I have often connected more easily with men, who are notorious for being emotionally unavailable. I feel most instinctively understood by Gen X women. Women who, like me, were raised to be capable, contained, and self-sufficient. Women who learned, early on, not to need too much.

That inheritance didn't begin with us. It came from mothers and grandmothers who defined themselves through duty and endurance. Women who survived by not complaining. Who loved through action more than affirmation. Who passed down a way of surviving that became a way of living - be strong, be useful, don't rely on anyone.

Now I find myself parenting alongside Millennials, a generation shaped by emotional connection and communal processing. When we gather, conversations often turn to anxiety, overwhelm, fear, and feelings, words I still feel almost allergic to naming, let alone sharing. And I realize that my discomfort isn't about them. It's about how easily they speak a language I was never taught.

My struggle to find that connection isn't a failure of care. It's a translation problem.

I don't want to coddle my daughter. But I also see the cost of the emotional distance I inherited, and carried, through different seasons of my life. Somewhere between my grandmother's endurance, my mother's restraint, and my daughter's emotional openness is a middle ground. And I am trying to live there.

I don't have all the answers, and I'm done pretending I do.

My daughter is eight and she seems fine. Better than fine, actually. She has boy and girl friends, she loves school, and she doesn't seem fazed by drama. Maybe I'm just projecting my shit onto her. She doesn't seem to be doing what I did at all or feeling left out in any way.

Last Friday night, Mia had a playdate with her best friend, a boy, from school. They played hide and seek, watched a movie, made up elaborate games that made no sense to me but had them both laughing until they couldn't breathe. They call each other best friends.

His mom and I are becoming friends too. She's someone I've really connected with and I'm excited about that. It feels rare and I'm trying not to worry about fucking it up.

Monday afternoon, I pulled up to the car line to pick Mia up from school. She was standing with a group of girls. When she saw my car, she nodded but before she could leave, three of them pulled her into a group hug.

She climbed into the back seat and handed me a folded piece of paper.

"Mom, Lilly asked for my phone number so I wrote down yours. She gave me her mom's too. Can you text her and set up a playdate? We really want to do something together."

I looked at her in the rearview mirror. "Of course, honey. That sounds like fun."

She has a boy best friend and girls who want her phone number and she doesn't seem confused about any of it. I wanted to feel relief and I did. But I also felt something else. Fear, maybe. Or just uncertainty.

She's the same age I was when the pool girls were already in their tight circle and I began to feel like the tag-along. This is the same age I was when I started watching from the sidelines instead of jumping in.

But she's not on the sidelines. She's in the middle of it. She has girls hugging her goodbye and boys calling her their best friend. She moves between both so easily.

I don't want to dump my baggage on her and see problems that aren't there. I don't want to turn her boy best friend into some warning sign because of what happened with me and my guy friends.

I hope she'll be fine. Maybe she won't repeat my patterns. Because I am trying to show up differently than my mom, maybe that's enough.

Or maybe it's not. She may hit 13 and suddenly the girl friendships will get complicated and she'll retreat to the boys because it's easier. Maybe she'll start walking away before anyone can leave her. I try not to wonder whether I'll watch her do exactly what I did and I won't know how to stop it.

I don't know yet, and that terrifies me.

For now, she's still a kid. She's happy and seems at ease.

I texted Lilly's mom and we set up a playdate for this weekend, and I'm trying not to worry about what comes next.

The teenage years terrify me. How do I keep from freaking out and passing my old insecurities onto her? What if I see her pull away from some friend group and I make it worse?

I see a difference between my childhood and hers. I'm more engaged in her life than my parents were in mine. We didn't talk about feelings at home. Kids learned to handle their shit on their own or with their friends. Now, I ask Mia about her day. I know her friends' names and their parents. I talk to her about race and current events and things my parents never talked to me about. I ask her how things make her feel. Maybe that's the difference and that's enough.

I've learned a few things writing this book. As much as it pains me to say, my mom and I are more alike than I wanted to admit. I spent years seeing her as weak, paralyzed by grief and depression, ultimately, dying alone. I told myself I would never be like her. But in reality, she had strength too. She survived losing everyone and she kept going even when she had nothing left. She ate nails for breakfast just like I did, we just showed it differently. I'm not better than her. I'm just her with more awareness.

Telling my story has made me feel lighter, like I can finally see it all clearly. The patterns, the fears, the way they moved through generations. Naming it doesn't mean I've fixed it, but at least I'm not pretending it's not there anymore.

And maybe that thing I've been searching for, that tribe of women all living near me, doing life together, maybe that was never realistic. Just maybe, I already have my tribe and it simply looks different than I imagined. Sarah is on the East Coast but she shows up when it matters. Amy doesn't need constant contact to stay close. Nancy, Diane and Lynn have been unexpected surprises in my life. Irwin chose me and keeps choosing me. Mia is watching me try. That's my tribe. It's small and it's spread out. It doesn't look like the Woodland Heights pool girls who still get together every year. But it's mine.

I still don't know if I'm protecting Mia or passing down damage. I still walk away from people before they can walk away from me. I still keep some of the moms I've met at arm's length. But I see it now, and I'm trying. Some days that feels like progress and others like I'm just aware of the pattern while I keep repeating it. I don't know which one it is. Maybe both.

What I do know is this. It's okay to not have all the answers. It's okay to be scared. It's okay to still be figuring it out at damn near 50. Me and my mom, who ate nails for breakfast, who survived everything, who never quite fit. Maybe we weren't broken. Maybe we were just trying our best with what we were given.

Book Playlist

These are the songs that carried me through writing this book. Some are from the years I'm writing about, the 90s hip hop and grunge that defined Gen X, the Dave Matthews Band concerts I went to, the Mary J. Blige I played on repeat after breakups.

I need to call out Alex Warren specifically. His music got me through the hardest parts of this process. He writes about grief and vulnerability in a way that gave me permission to do the same. When I couldn't find the words for what I was feeling, his songs held space for it. Mia and I listen to him together now, and that feels like its own kind of healing.

You can find the full playlist on Spotify: *Nails for Breakfast*

What About Your Friends - TLC
None of Your Business - Salt-N-Pepa
Closer to Fine - Indigo Girls

Head Over Feet - Alanis Morissette

U.N.I.T.Y. - Queen Latifah

Weak - SWV

You Learn - Alanis Morissette

End of the Road - Boys II Men

Creep - TLC

Black - Pearl Jam

With or Without You - U2

What Would You Say - Dave Matthews Band

Go Your Own Way - Fleetwood Mac

Time After Time - Cyndi Lauper

Don't Drink the Water - Dave Matthews Band

Personal Jesus - Depeche Mode

Everybody Wants to Rule the World - Tears for Fears

Eternity - Alex Warren

Carry You Home - Alex Warren

Save You a Seat - Alex Warren

Give You Love - Alex Warren

You'll Be Alright, Kid - Alex Warren

The Best - Nicotine Dolls

Let It Go - James Bay

See You Again (feat. Charlie Puth) - Wiz Khalifa,
    Charlie Puth

A Lot More Free - Max McNown

Crash Into Me - Dave Matthews Band

Fix You - Coldplay

Who I Am - Alex Warren

100 Bad Days - AJR

It Takes Two - Rob Base & DJ EZ Rock

Jump Around - House of Pain

Hip Hop Hooray - Naughty By Nature

Poison - Bell Biv DeVoe

Informer - Snow

Let Me Clear My Throat - DJ Kool

Not Gon' Cry - Mary J. Blige

Before You Leave Me - Alex Warren

Glitter In the Air - Pink

A Change Is Gonna Come - Sam Cooke

When I Get There - Pink

The Story - Brandi Carlile

Demons - Imagine Dragons

Take Me to Church - Hozier

Hallelujah - Jeff Buckley

Bless the Broken Road - Rascal Flatts

Hangin' Tough - New Kids On The Block

Fast Car - Tracy Chapman

My Girl - The Temptations

Black and Yellow - Wiz Khalifa

I Can Do It With a Broken Heart - Taylor Swift

Three Steps Ahead - Jared Benjamin

Rescue - Lauren Daigle

Stay With Me - Sam Smith

Ordinary - Alex Warren

Where or When - Wynton Marsalis

No Scrubs - TLC

Torn - Natalie Imbruglia

Stay - Lisa Loeb

I Found - Amber Run

Family Portrait - Pink

Summertime - DJ Jazzy Jeff

Day 'N' Nite - Kid Cudi

You Are the Best Thing - Ray LaMontagne

Rise Up - Andra Day

Scan to listen on Spotify:

Acknowledgments

To Erin Donley: You knew me when I was the young girl at the pool and on the tennis court, and now, decades later, you became my writing coach and helped me tell this story. You sat with me through every draft and doubt. You helped me see the patterns I couldn't name and find my voice when I was drowning in everyone else's. Thank you for proving that maybe I was wrong about not belonging all those years ago.

To Michael LaRocca: Thank you for your detailed eye in proofreading and for treating these words with such care.

To Shiloh Schroeder: Thank you for the cover, the layout and for making my vision come to life.

To Irwin: You saw my patterns and stayed anyway. You chose me when I was still learning how to be chosen. You gave me space to write this book, to build a business, to figure out who

I am without the armor. Thank you for rewriting everything I thought I knew about love. Love you.

To Mia: You're my greatest gift and teacher. Watching you navigate friendship, race, and belonging with more grace than I ever had at your age humbles me daily. I'm still figuring out how to see you clearly through my own damage. Thank you for your patience while I try. Love you babygirl.

To Sarah, Amy, Drew, Diane, Nancy, and Lynn: You each showed up in different ways, at different times, when I needed you most. Together, you proved that the tribe I was looking for doesn't have to look like I imagined. You're my people. Thank you.

To Patrick: I'm sorry I didn't call. I'm sorry I waited until it was too late. I miss you.

To the pool girls who sent that wind chime when my mom died: That one gesture made me question everything I believed about fitting in. Maybe I was wrong about all of it. Thank you for making me rethink the story I'd been telling myself.

To my Mom and Dad: I know I wasn't always easy growing up. I'm grateful for the hard seasons and the fun ones too. You both shaped me into the woman I am today, and while I'm still working on being better, I think I turned out pretty okay. I love you and miss you both. I hope you're enjoying your Friday night date nights wherever you are.

To everyone else who touched my life and shows up in these pages: The ones who hurt me, the ones I hurt, the ones I walked away from, the ones who walked away from me - thank you for the lessons. The hard ones especially. Those are the ones that made the book.

Author Bio

Chrissy Liu has never done anything the expected way.

She earned her law degree from the University of Pittsburgh, studied bioethics in Rome, and spent exactly one year practicing law before deciding it wasn't her life. What followed was 15 years as a healthcare administrator at some of the country's leading institutions - Children's National Medical Center and George Washington University Cancer Center in Washington DC, Duke Cancer Institute in Durham, North Carolina, and Fred Hutch/University of Washington in Seattle.

After leaving healthcare, she founded Chrissy Liu Jewelry. Her work was featured in national magazines and sold in stores and museums across the country. She built something from nothing, the way she always had, and walked away when her body told her it was time.

Eating Nails for Breakfast is her debut memoir. Her first novel is in progress.

Chrissy lives in Colorado with her husband Irwin, her daughter and her two dogs. She is a Pittsburgh Steelers fan, a recovering attorney, a former jeweler, and a woman who is still, at nearly 50, figuring out where she fits.

Find me at www.chrissyliu.com for book club resources, upcoming projects, and to connect.

www.ingramcontent.com/pod-product-compliance
Lightning Source LLC
Chambersburg PA
CBHW031129130726
47988CB00006B/2287